D0506458

ALADDIN "BUILT IN A DAY" HOUSE CATALOG, 1917

The Aladdin Company

DOVER PUBLICATIONS, INC.
New York

Copyright

Published in Canada by General Publishing Company, Ltd., 30 Lesmill Road, Don Mills, Toronto, Ontario.
Published in the United Kingdom by Constable and Company, Ltd., 3 The Lanchesters, 162–164 Fulham Palace Road, London W6 9ER.

Bibliographical Note

The present edition, first published by Dover Publications, Inc., in 1995, is an unabridged republication of *Aladdin Homes "Built in a Day" Catalog No. 29, 1917*, published by The Aladdin Company in Bay City, Michigan. Some pages have been rearranged for this edition. Some illustrations originally appeared in color.

Library of Congress Cataloging-in-Publication Data

Aladdin Company.
[Aladdin homes "built in a day"]
Aladdin "built in a day" house catalog, 1917 / the Aladdin Company.
p. cm.
"The present edition, first published in 1995, is an unabridged republication of Aladdin homes 'built in a day' catalog no. 29, 1917, published by the Aladdin Company in Bay City, Michigan"—T.p. verso.
ISBN 0-486-28591-X
1. Prefabricated houses—United States—Catalogs. I. Title.
NA8480.A6 1995
728'.37'0222—dc20 95-2395
CIP

Manufactured in the United States of America
Dover Publications, Inc., 31 East 2nd Street, Mineola, N.Y. 11501

ALADDIN HOMES

Manufactured by
THE ALADDIN COMPANY
of Bay City, Michigan

ALADDIN Offices at Bay City, Michigan.

THE ALADDIN COMPANY

BAY CITY, MICH.

OFFICE OF
O.E. Sovereign
Secretary - Treasurer
General Manager.

Dear Friend :-

After you have selected the Aladdin Home you like best, you will want to know more about it than can be told in this catalog.

And we have many interesting things to tell you, too. We'll send you a more complete description of all the materials. We'll send you estimates on the cost of shipping, erection and completion; and our Service Department will write you of the many ways we have to help you finish your home.

But first, you must write us which house you are interested in. In the meantime, if you will refer to the index of subjects on this page, you will find reference to many interesting facts covered in this catalog.

We anticipate the pleasure of working with you to the end that your home will be completed in a way that is pleasurable and satisfactory.

Inviting an early letter, we are

Cordially yours,

Otto E. Sovereign

Sec'y, Treas. & Gen'l Mgr.

Index of Subjects

Evidence of Aladdin's Leadership

ALADDIN has been honored the past two or three years in different ways, but is most proud of the medals awarded by two great expositions. The Panama-Pacific International Exposition, that most wonderful of all great World's Fairs, and the Michigan Agricultural Exposition granted "Les Grandes Prix," issuing diplomas as shown in photographs. The Panama-Pacific Medal was issued upon the Model Cottage which Aladdin produced and erected for Uncle Sam, while the Michigan Exposition Medal was the result of our building a Kentucky bungalow at the fair for the Northeastern Michigan Development Bureau. Official record is made in the Diploma that The Aladdin Company originated, perfected and established the Readi-Cut System of Construction. These facts are quoted here merely as additional evidence of Aladdin's leadership in all things pertaining to Scientific Home Building. But the greatest test of leadership is the universal record of satisfaction to our customers.

State of Michigan

Whereas, It is the province of the Michigan Agricultural Society to recognize and assist in advancing all improvements both along Agricultural and Industrial lines; and

Whereas, The conservation of time and material in the construction of buildings is distinctly along the line of such advancement; and

Whereas, The Aladdin house constructed by The Aladdin Company for the Northeastern Michigan Development Bureau, which house has been recently erected on the grounds of the Michigan Agricultural Society, is a strong demonstration of saving of expense in building by scientific, practical, economical and successful conservation of material; in the elimination of waste in both material and labor; and

Whereas, The Aladdin Company originated, perfected and established the Readi-Cut System of Construction, therefore be it

Resolved, That the Michigan Agricultural Society does hereby award to The Aladdin Company a certificate of merit consisting of a Gold Medal suitably inscribed, and the same is hereby authorized.

Dated Sept 8 1914

G. W. Dickinson
Secretary and Manager

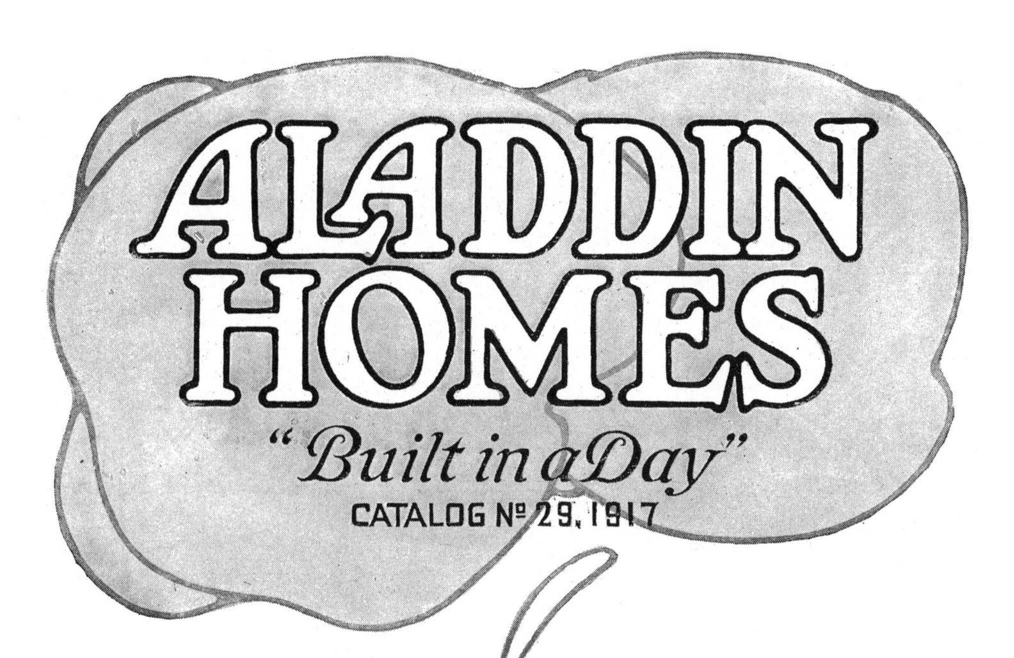

THE ALADDIN COMPANY

Previously the

NORTH AMERICAN CONSTRUCTION CO.

W. J. Sovereign..............................Pres.

O. E. Sovereign,...Sec.Treas.Gen.Mgr.

General Offices, Bay City, Mich.

IMPORTANT: Read the following introductory pages carefully.

Complete houses shipped direct from our mills in Michigan, Louisiana, Oregon, Florida, U. S. A., and Toronto, Ottawa and Vancouver, Canada

Address all communications direct to home offices at Bay City, Michigan. Cable Address: "Aladdin," Western Union code

Canadian Branch: Sovereign Construction Co., C. P. R. Bldg., Toronto, Ontario

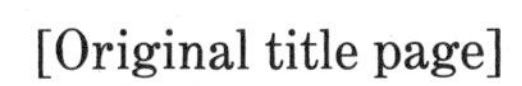

[Original title page]

Center sill foundation timber cut to fit.
Joists, studding, rafters, and ceiling joists all accurately cut to fit.
Sheathing lumber cut to fit. Sub-floors cut to fit.
Joist bridging cut to fit.
Building paper for all dwellings for side walls and floor linings.
All bevel siding, every single piece guaranteed to be cut and to fit accurately.
Shingles or siding for the side walls, whichever preferred, will be furnished for any house at no additional cost.
Outside finishing lumber, all cut to fit.
Flooring, cut to fit. Roof sheathing, cut to fit.
Porch timbers, joists, flooring, columns, railing and posts, moulding, roof sheathing, all and every piece cut to fit except porch rail, uncut.
Extra Star-A-Star Cedar Shingles or prepared roofing.
Outside steps of all dwellings cut and shaped to fit.
All doors mortised and with frame and trim inside and out. Windows and frame, sash, and glass, and trim inside and out.
Moulded base board for rooms, not cut to fit.
Weather moulding for trimming all outside doors and windows, cut to fit. Crown mould, cove mould and quarter round mould, etc.
Stairways, treads, risers, stringers, newel posts, balusters, moulding, etc., for all two-story houses cut to fit. .
All hardware. Mortise locks, knobs, and hinges, tin flashing, hip shingles, galvanized ridge roll, window hardware, etc.
Nails of proper size for entire house.
Paint for two coats outside body and trim (any colors), putty, oils, stains, and varnishes.
Lath and plaster and grounds or plaster board for lining entire house.
Complete instructions and illustrations for doing all the work.
(Aladdin houses are always shipped under the freight classification of lumber with hardware, etc., listed under their respective classifications. See page 10.)
The floor plan of any house in this catalog will be reversed without extra charge.

TERMS

TWENTY-FIVE per cent. cash with order, balance C. O. D. This is not meant as a reflection on your financial standing, but is an invariable rule. A discount of 5% is allowed from list prices where full amount is sent with order. For your convenience, we have shown the list price and the net price with each house.

An illustration: List price of house, $1,000, 25% cash with order—$250, balance $750 C. O. D., or 5% discount for sending full amount — 5%, $50 from $1,000—$950, if all sent with order. You save $50 by sending full amount with order on a $1,000 house, other houses same in proportion. Cash discount is often large enough to pay freight charges.

THE ALADDIN COMPANY

General Offices, Bay City, Michigan

REFERENCES: Any Bank in the United States, Bradstreet's or Dun's Commercial Agencies, First National Bank of Bay City, Michigan; The Chemical National Bank, New York City; The First National Bank of Chicago, and The First and Old Detroit National Bank of Detroit, any city official or other citizen of Bay City, and our customers.

ALADDIN READI-CUT HOUSES Sold By The GOLDEN RULE

Address all communications Direct to Home Office at Bay City, Michigan.

Highest Award World's Fair

[Original copyright page]

The Aladdin Plan

This is the Twelfth Year of Aladdin Success

ALADDIN Readi-Cut Houses—the Aladdin System of Construction—may be new to *you,* but the system was planned and put in operation twelve years ago. Its merit, its wonderful simplicity, was immediately recognized by the American public. The result is that each year the history of the business shows a doubling and trebling in the volume and number of houses sold. You know that this wonderful growth would be impossible for any manufacturing institution, or any business house, unless customers became friends — unless real *service* was rendered—honest value, square business methods, and integrity prevailed.

Integrity of the Aladdin Policy

Integrity means *moral soundness;* it means *honesty;* it means *freedom from corrupting influence or practice;* it means *strictness in the fulfillment of contracts, uprightness, square dealing.* The Aladdin policy of doing business endeavors to live up to the strictest meaning of *Integrity.* The customer must be well served—must be satisfied—must be pleased—*must be a friend.* The *Golden Rule* must govern every transaction. You who read this are entitled to know the truth of the above statement. Well, then, demand of us that proof in whatever way you wish. Shall we give you bankers, congressmen, postmasters, city, State or National Government officials, or, better than all, shall we refer you to *customers who have tested our integrity,* customers in your own neighborhood? The proof is yours for the asking.

The Aladdin System of Construction is Built on This Principle:

Modern power-driven machines can do BETTER *work at a lower cost than hand labor. Then every bit of work that* CAN *be done by machines* SHOULD *be so done.* The steel worker with a little hack-saw trying to cut and fit the steel girders of the modern skyscraper should be no more out of place than the modern carpenter cutting sills, joists, and rafters. The skyscraper framework is cut to fit by machines in the steel mills, marked and numbered ready for erection. The lumber in the Aladdin house is cut to fit by machines in the Aladdin mills, marked and numbered ready for erection. The steel system is twenty-five years old—the Aladdin system twelve years old.

BEFORE this Board of Seven comes every Aladdin house for the acid test of perfection. No detail escapes the keen and searching analysis of these experts. The designer must prove his plans to the complete satisfaction of, First, the Master Designer, for accuracy; Second, the Master Builders, for practicability, strength, and structural harmony; Third, Factory Experts, for elimination of waste, standardization of lengths, and economy of costs. Unless the cost of these high-priced men's time could be spread over a hundred or more houses of each design the cost would be prohibitive. But when they spend two or more hours' valuable time on the design, drawings, and cutting sheets of an Aladdin house the cost is not all charged to that *one house,* but to *several hundred* houses of that *same design* sold during the year.

No other organization — but the Aladdin organization — can afford a group of high-calibred men such as this Board of Seven, because no other organization in the world produces and sells the vast number of houses and buildings produced by The Aladdin Company.

No other organization can afford to put such high quality into its goods—and no other organization does.

No other lumber manufacturer ever dared back his lumber with a dollar-a-knot guarantee.

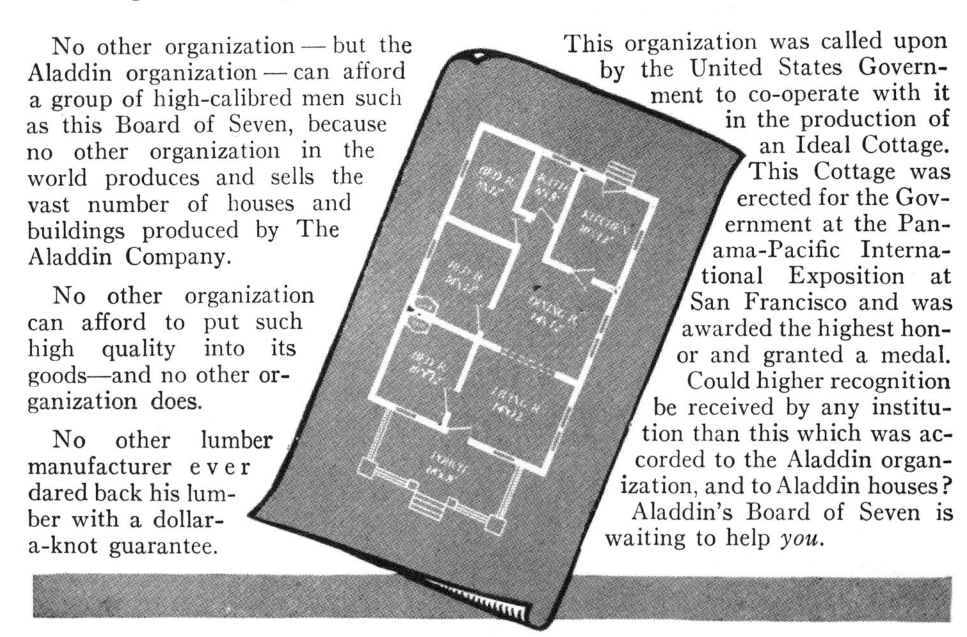

This organization was called upon by the United States Government to co-operate with it in the production of an Ideal Cottage. This Cottage was erected for the Government at the Panama-Pacific International Exposition at San Francisco and was awarded the highest honor and granted a medal. Could higher recognition be received by any institution than this which was accorded to the Aladdin organization, and to Aladdin houses? Aladdin's Board of Seven is waiting to help *you.*

Twenty feet of lumber from a sixteen foot board How it's done

To cut the sheathing for this gable:

The carpenter usually takes an eight-foot board, a six-foot board, a four-foot board and a two-foot board and cuts them this way:

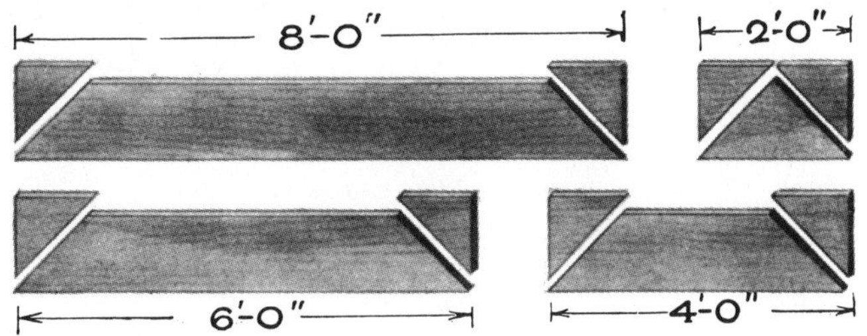

The carpenter requires twenty feet of lumber for the job. Aladdin takes a sixteen-foot board, cuts it this way:

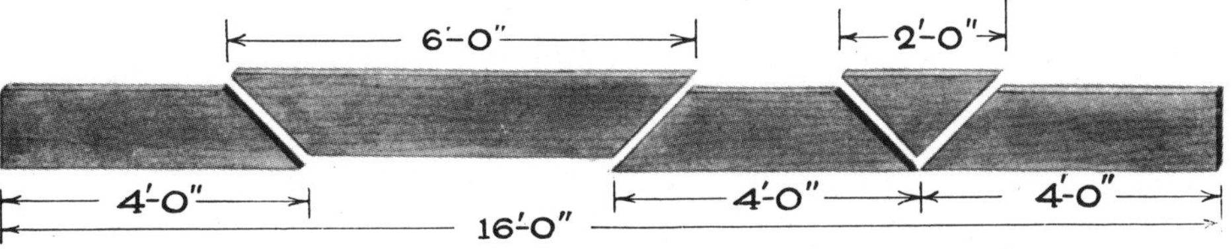

and gets twenty feet of lumber at the cost of sixteen feet—and YOU get the saving.

THE wonderful money saving results of the Aladdin Readi-Cut System will be understood after reading this page. Nowhere in the history of manufacturing or building since history began can be found an example equal to that which is a part of every day's work in the Aladdin designing rooms and in the Aladdin mills.

Machinery of the Most Modern types are used to manufacture Aladdin Homes. This machine houses and fits a staircase in less than five minutes.

Think of taking a six-inch board sixteen feet long and getting twenty feet of six-inch board out of it!

Think of applying this *system of saving* throughout *all* the lumber used in building *your* home!

Think of your own good money *it saves!*

To eliminate waste by scientific planning, designing, and cutting of lumber is to save *your* money from the waste pile.

W. J. Sovereign, president of The Aladdin Company, conceived this tremendous thought, originated, perfected, and established the system. Imitators have been many the past three or four years, but not one has yet even approached Aladdin efficiency, nor has one yet established a success. It took six years of Aladdin success before any one had the courage to even attempt to manufacture houses in the footsteps of this company.

WASTE—and what it Means to You

"Big Ben": The most wonderful woodworking machine ever built. It does the work of 100 men every day.

"Only Thirty-five per cent of the original tree emerges in the form of a building."—SATURDAY EVENING POST.

SPECIAL investigation of waste in the construction of dwellings resulted in the following statement by a writer in the *Retail Lumberman:*

"A safe estimate of good lumber wasted in course of construction is 25%."

These two bare statements are quoted from such unquestionable sources to give especial weight to our very conservative statement:

You will pay for 18% waste when you build the old *way.*

Eighteen per cent of your money will pay for material *you don't get*—eighteen dollars out of every hundred spent in your home—wasted.

When this statement was first made by us it was ridiculed by the lumbermen. The passing years have wrought changes in their ideas until now, when pinned down, they will admit that it is conservative.

We have reduced the item of waste to less than 2%.

The architect, in designing a house, seldom considers the subject of cutting material to waste. He lays out the dimensions of the house, places windows, doors, etc., without any thought of how the material will cut. The contractor orders so many thousand feet of siding, of flooring, of 2 x 4, of 2 x 6, etc., without any thought as to the utilization of mill-run lengths. You, of course, know that sawmills cut logs in certain lengths, 10 feet, 12 feet, 14 feet and 16 feet, and it comes through the planing mill in those same lengths. It also comes to the contractor in the same lengths. When the carpenter cuts the siding to fit between two windows, the windows may be 10 feet 1 inch apart. He has to take 14 pieces of siding each 12 feet long and cut each one of them 10 feet 1 inch, wasting 1 foot 11 inches, or about 18% of good lumber absolutely wasted. The principle is the same throughout the entire house.

This waste is eliminated by the Aladdin designers and the Aladdin Readi-Cut system.

Our buyers go actually into the woods, confer with the owners and cutters of the timber and buy the right lengths that will come out of the woods, through the sawmills and into our own mills in the right lengths. We don't take raw material in lengths and sizes as it chances to come, but as *it should come to conform to our standards.* In many instances the cross-cut saw in the hands of the woodsman is actually directed by our needs so that no other saw is touched to the lumber at any time.

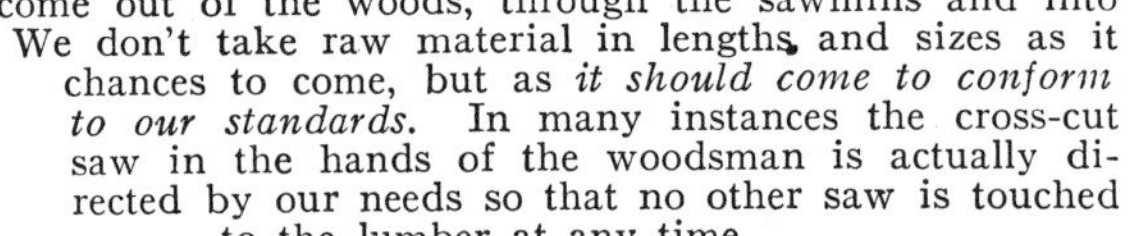

Each one of our special gang cut-off saws is designed to cut 50,000 feet of studding and joists every day. It does the work that would require a veritable army of carpenters to do, and it does it with the wonderful perfection and accuracy of high-class machinery.

You can easily imagine the dollars saved to *you* in the cost of *your* home, accomplished by this remarkable system; a system of *saving waste* that reaches into the very forest and untiringly searches every item, every operation, every movement to cut out and to eliminate the waste of *your money.*

When the architect overlooks something or makes a mistake, *you* pay the bill; when the contractor overlooks something, or makes a mistake, *you* pay for that, too; and when the carpenter uses poor judgment, overlooks something or makes a mistake, *you are the one to stand the cost of his mistake.* It's always your money—not the other's.

The more brains, the more organization, the more counsel given to any matter the less chance for mistakes, and the Aladdin Board of Seven, described on another page, is *your* safeguard.

From the Pyramids to the Woolworth Building

TO him who says the Readi-Cut System is not possible or practicable, point to the Pyramids of Egypt, refer to Solomon's Temple as described in the Bible, or inspect Washington Monument, or the 57-story Woolworth Building in New York City. You will find that each was prepared, erected and completed by the Readi-Cut System. But it remained for W. J. Sovereign to first apply the system to *your* benefit in the building of a home. And thousands of American families scattered over this broad land will testify to its economy and practical success.

The pyramids aren't portable, the Woolworth Building is not portable, *nor are Aladdin* houses portable.

If you attempted to tear apart, or dissect an Aladdin house, the most expert contractor could not tell it from any other first class frame dwelling because *there is no difference.*

At the bottom of this page is a striking illustration of the Readi-Cut System of construction successfully used for twenty-five years in steel-building construction. Note the "studding" for the two side walls, all in position with the "joist hanger" placed. These studs are about thirty feet high. In the foreground are shown some of the rafters, with the marks and numbers indicating their respective positions—"6201-16-Col-22." There is no fitting or cutting on the ground. The sawing, measuring, and fitting were done in the steel mills in Pittsburgh. How can they do this work? Why, the structural engineers know how. It's their particular business. It's their life-work. So it is with Aladdin Readi-Cut houses. The same *principles* govern each job. *It's the same system.*

Readi-Cut System of Construction.

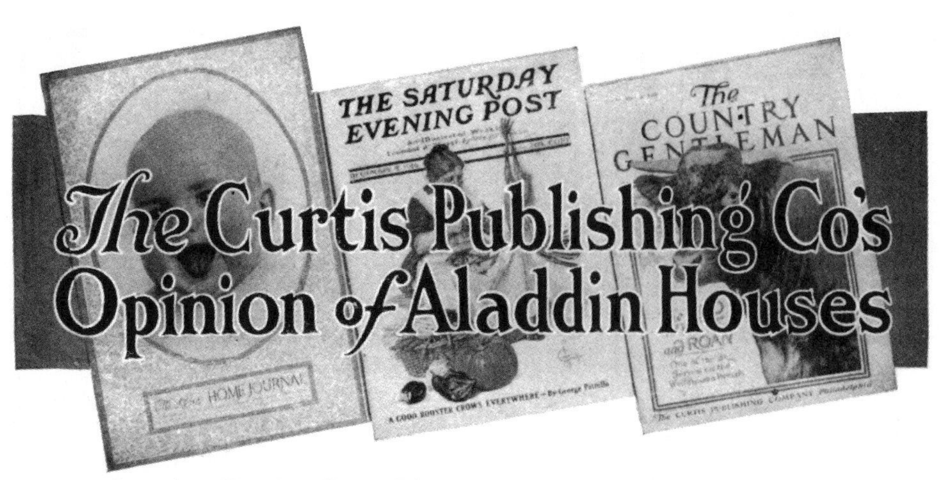

The Saturday Evening Post, The Ladies' Home Journal and The Country Gentleman are owned and published by the Curtis Publishing Co., of Philadelphia. The following statement was written, signed and published by them:

"Today Aladdin's houses stand in every part of the world, from Saskatchewan to the Tahiti Islands, in hot and cold climates. There are whole communities built of Aladdin houses. As many as 200 homes have been sold in three months to the same purchasers—large industrial concerns which house their own employes. In the offices 120 girls are employed to handle the correspondence, which has amounted to more than 300,000 pieces of mail in one month. The business is growing tremendously. The lumber mills (some of which it owns) are working at top speed, producing forty houses a day, at prices ranging from $138 to $8,000 each."

And this from "The Canada Lumberman"

"Year after year the price of carpenter labor has been advancing, thus making the cost of lumber higher when in position. Framing material will eventually have to come to the building trimmed to length, and I fail to understand why this fact is not more generally realized. The piece stuff of the future will be furnished to the building ready for position. This thing of cutting and cutting with a handsaw at the building site until it fits, is too costly."

Largest conveyor of finished lumber in the world. It does the work of many men and horses.

The United States Government

has given to The Aladdin Company, the right to apply to its product (Aladdin Houses) *"Sold By the Golden Rule."* It has given the Company the *Exclusive Right,* backed up by all the patent laws. This recognition, this rare privilege, we are immensely proud of.

This Catalog Our Only Salesman

With this catalog, you are able to keep the profits in your own pocket that you would ordinarily pay to your local dealers. Because we do not sell thru dealers, they can't add their four or five hundred dollar profits to the goods you buy from us. You *keep* this money *yourself.*

When your dealer says "Don't buy your lumber out of town," ask him where *he* buys the lumber he wants to sell you.

You see he buys his lumber up here and the only money that stays in your town is the *dealer's profit.* Wouldn't you rather have it in your pocket, than in his?

This catalog makes possible this saving—and many others. Pick the house that meets *your* need, and write us. We have lots of interesting things to tell you about it.

Every piece of framing and sheathing lumber in every Aladdin house has been carefully selected from the highest grade. Clear and knotless Oregon Fir and Yellow Pine is used for all inside finish at the Bay City mills. From our Florida and Louisiana mills we use yellow pine. From our Oregon mill we ship all material in Fir. It is carefully inspected by experienced men, and if not up to a high standard is not used. This is an extremely important point and you should consider it carefully. Our facilities for buying high grades are unequaled by any manufacturer of lumber in the country. This means much to the purchaser—to know the quality of all materials used, to know that the lumber and timber are the best; that it is well seasoned, sound, and of first quality throughout.

All the interior finish, doors, etc., are put through three separate sanding machines, making a beautiful finish.

Scores have written, "It would have been impossible to obtain locally, finish at any price to equal that furnished in my Aladdin." [Such names and addresses gladly furnished on request.]

What You Get When You Buy an Aladdin House

Material that is not equalled by any other concern in the country, and it is not only perfectly cut to fit, but cut with a view of saving all waste which means a direct saving to you. But the saving does not stop there. We mortise all doors to receive the lock sets, all interior finish sanded, and flooring steel scraped.

Shingle Mountain, over 20 Million Shingles in the Aladdin Yards.

Bear in mind that when you buy an Aladdin house that the foundation sill, floor joists, the sub flooring, the regular tongued and grooved flooring, the studding, the wall sheathing, the siding, the window and door frames, the outside finish, the rafters, the roof sheathing, the steps, the stairs, all porch framing, is *readi-cut,* ready to nail into place. Just think, is it any wonder that we can save you such a big percentage of your labor cost. And then again the enormous quantities in which we buy our building paper, lock sets, double acting door hinges, window weights, nails, paints, varnishes, oils, stains, hip shingles, tin flashing, etc., sets them down at your door for less than a hardware dealer can buy them from the jobber.

Direct from the Forest to the Home

Stop and think what that means—"direct from the forest to you." It means that you are buying your house at the same price it costs if you lived right here—right where the timber grows—to build a house. It means that your house costs you no more than if you could go direct to a mill at the edge of the forest and buy the timber and lumber. It means that you are really doing that very thing—buying it from the mill at the edge of the forest. It means that you are *not* paying a profit to the big *jobber,* a profit to the big *wholesaler,* and a profit to the local *lumber dealer* at your home, and, on top of all that, the freight for shipping the lumber to the several places where each does business. The house is shipped to you "direct from the forest to the home." Another thing, each of the above lumber dealers, or middlemen, sells on credit. They all add from 5% to 10% to make up for bad accounts—losses which are charged up in your bill. We sell for cash only—we have no bad accounts, and are, therefore, not obliged to add enough charges into your bill to make up for the man who doesn't pay.

"I'll Pay $1.00 for Every Knot"

any customer can find in our Red Cedar Siding shipped from Bay City. I stand ready to prove to you in this way that the lumber in Aladdin Readi-Cut Houses is Higher in grade throughout than is regularly carried by any seller of lumber in America. Clear and Knotless Siding, Clear and Knotless Flooring, Clear and Knotless Interior Finish, Clear and Knotless Shingles, and Clear and Knotless Outside Finish, are furnished for every Aladdin Dwelling House. Every piece of exposed lumber on Aladdin houses in 1915 and 1916 was Clear and Knotless and will be *Clear and Knotless* in 1917. **O. E. SOVEREIGN, Gen. Mgr., The Aladdin Company.**

Aladdin's Famous "Dollar-A-Knot" Guaranty

A NEW standard of lumber quality has been given to the world by Aladdin's famous "Dollar-A-Knot" Guaranty.

The "Good-enough" lumber grades, the "Anything-will-do" grades and the multitudes of evasive substitutions for Clear Knotless lumber have been shown up.

You cannot be expected to fathom the intricacies of lumber associations' manual of grading rules; how many circles, hearts, rings and barks make a good log, nor how many knots, spots, pitch pockets or worm holes there will be to a board.

There are none of these defects in your dollar, and there should be none in what you trade your dollar for.

Knotless Means Just What It Says

"A dollar a knot!" Could any guaranty be plainer, or more forceful, or more effective? You know a knot when you see it, and you know it makes a board less valuable. And when we guarantee Aladdin lumber to be knotless or guarantee "A Dollar-A-Knot" you *know* that your lumber is going to be the very *highest* grade taken from the forest.

"Hunting for Pieces"—Contractor

Of course, the Aladdin Readi-Cut System receives adverse criticism from some contractors, lumber dealers, and others. This criticism comes chiefly from those who have had no experience with or knowledge of Aladdin houses. Self-interest, here prompted by loss of profit, begets the antagonism.

One of the most amusing remarks made is that the builder of an Aladdin house will lose as much time hunting out his material and finding the right piece as he will save by the Readi-Cut System. Of course, this remark on the face of it is an admission that time is saved by the Aladdin System. However, any thought about time lost in hunting for pieces is immediately dispelled when you see the simple system of laying out materials that accompanies the instructions for every house.

About Freight

One of the big advantages in buying an Aladdin house is the big amount you save on the item of freight alone. Your local dealer very rarely buys his lumber from the forest. He gets it shipped to him from his wholesaler at some near-by distributing point. The wholesaler usually gets it from some other middleman, who gets it from the sawmill. Every time the lumber is moved in its zigzag course through the middlemen, the freight charges pile up and your local dealer must add them all into the price you pay. When *your Aladdin house* reaches you the freight is the very lowest that is possible to move the goods to your station. It reaches you in a straight line from the forest. We use great care in quoting the freight and great care in routing it the most direct way. It costs no more to pay the freight upon arrival of your car than to send us the money with which to prepay it.

Lath and Plaster or Aladdin Plaster Board—Your Choice

You may choose either lath and plaster or Aladdin plaster board for your interior walls. Our plaster is the highest grade manufactured and never fails to give the best results; a hard, smooth and lasting wall, is quick drying and impervious to moisture.

Aladdin plaster board is easily and quickly put on; its construction gives protection against extremes in weather; it is fireproof. It will not crack with age, nor loosen from dampness.

It comes in sheets 32x36 in. in size and is nailed directly to the studding.

We also furnish a special Plasto-filler, which, when mixed with water, is used to fill all joints of the plaster board, or, as we sometimes recommend, you can put a putty coat or hard-plaster finish directly onto the board.

We will furnish either lath and plaster or plaster board, whichever is specified by the customer.

The plaster that we furnish is an improved wood fibre patent plaster. This does away with the work of preparing plaster through the old fashioned method. It not only shortens the labor but when the wall is finished it is a great deal more durable and less liable to pit. It also effects another saving as the time required to set and dry out is much shorter, so that the interior finish can be put on without the usual delay.

For quick work or for use in cold weather it is preferable to any other plaster as it will set and harden much more rapidly.

Painting

With every Aladdin house, paint of any color for two coats outside is furnished, oils, stains, and varnishes or paints for inside. You will be sent, on request, our large color card of many beautiful colors. You may select as many different colors as you wish to choose for body, trimmings, porch floor, porch ceiling, window sash, etc., and you may have either paint, oil and varnish, stain and varnish, or stain and wax, for the interior finish. Where houses are furnished with shingles for the side walls, shingle stain is furnished instead of paint.

Masonry

Of course, all excavation and masonry work must be done on the ground. No money would be saved by including stone or brick or concrete, for every section of the country produces this material and prices vary but little. We furnish you with the foundation plan and will give you figures on the amount of material required for whatever kind of foundation material you decide to use—concrete, stone or brick. Fireplaces or chimneys may be built inside or outside and placed wherever desired or omitted. The opening for the chimney is not cut, so that the chimney may be omitted or its location changed from wherever it may be shown in our photographs.

Aladdin Houses Sold by the Golden Rule

Ten years of square dealing with our customers earned for us the expression, "I know that you do business very much on the *Golden Rule* basis."

This came in the mail voluntarily from a customer who had tested our business principles over a period of several years, and who has reason to know whereof he speaks. This principle has been governing the work of this organization constantly, and it is surely gratifying to have it come to us in this way.

We have, therefore, adopted the expression and know that we have a real right to its use—as *you* will know when you join the big Aladdin family.

General Specifications

IMPORTANT NOTE.—The pictures shown in this catalog are all actual photographs of Aladdin houses sent to us by our customers. There are no fanciful artists' drawings, or photographs of houses not built the Aladdin way. Every house shown in this catalog is erected in Bay City, the home of Aladdin, with just two or three exceptions. *This cannot be said of any other similar catalog.*

No single organization in the world ever equalled the vast experience of this institution in the designing and manufacturing of houses. The shipment of thousands of houses each year and covering a period of twelve years *at this work* means exact knowledge—not theory—on the subject of *material and construction.* The grades of material, the sizes of timbers, their strength, location and installation in the building are determined by well defined engineering standards and our own exact knowledge gained from years of experience.

Below are given general specifications for the construction of Aladdin houses. The exact specifications for the house of your choice are sent you without cost *just as soon as you write us* about the house you like best.

Quantities

A binding guaranty is given to furnish sufficient material for the completion of each house in accordance with the specifications that follow.

Condition of Material

The company pledges itself to deliver your house to you without damage in shipment, or in transit. Anything damaged on arrival will be instantly made good *at our expense.*

Sizes of Timbers

All sizes of all timbers and lumber will be in accordance with well established engineering and architectural standards of safety and strength.

Quality of Material

All lumber is guaranteed to be of the highest grades ever marketed anywhere in the world. Every Aladdin house, regardless of size or price, comes under this binding guaranty. (Exception: Sheathing lumber is a fine No. 2 quality, and far better than the accepted standard for sheathing lumber.)

General Detail Specifications

Foundation.—Material for foundation is, of course, not included with Aladdin houses, as concrete, stone or brick can be secured in one locality as cheaply as in another. Complete foundation plans are furnished you with detailed instructions for buying this material and building your foundation.

Sills.—Center sill, or sills, are, of course, always furnished to set into your foundation of concrete, stone or brick. All sills are of a size to amply hold all strains and loads in accordance with engineering standards and good practice.

Joists.—All framed, dressed and cut to fit. All joists are of a size to amply hold all strains and loads in accordance with engineering standards and good practice.

Flooring.—The flooring used in Aladdin Houses is clear and knotless, tongued and grooved, matched fir flooring. It has a beautifully figured grain. The face is steel scraped to give the very best appearance.

Bridgings.—Wood bridging mitred and cut to length furnished for joists of first and second stories of all dwelling houses.

Sub-Floors (for both first and second stories in all Aladdin dwellings).—Inch lumber, dressed, all cut to fit.

Studding.—Size, 2x4 inches, all framed, dressed and cut to fit and placed on 16-inch centers.

Wall Sheathing.—Inch lumber, all dressed and cut to fit.

Rafters.—Size, 2x4 and 2x6 inches, all framed, mitred and beveled, dressed and, of course, guaranteed to be perfectly cut to fit.

Roof Sheathing.—Inch lumber, all framed, mitred, beveled, dressed and guaranteed to be cut to fit perfectly.

Shingles (Roof).—Extra Star A Star Cedar.

Building Paper.—Pure White Fibre, tough

and dense, for side walls and between subfloors and finished floors of all Aladdin dwellings.

Side Walls—Dollar-A-Knot Cedar siding, every piece cut to fit perfectly; perfectly machined surface and without sap, stain or any defects. Holds paint perfectly. Shingles for side walls instead of siding will be furnished for any Aladdin dwelling without extra charge.

Porch Columns.—All Colonial columns and square columns are of clear material and built with a lock-joint.

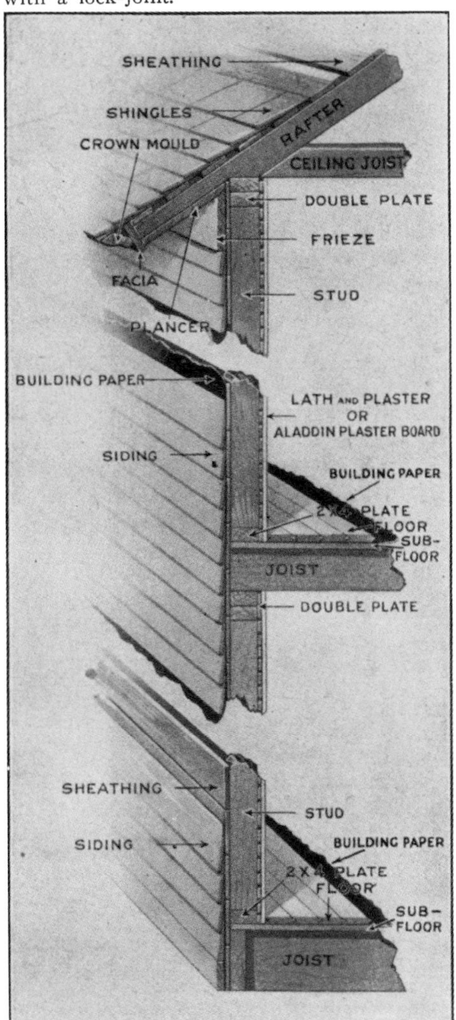

Outside Finish.—All outside finish is of clear and Knotless Yellow Pine or Fir.

Window and Door Frames.—Complete, including jams, casings, stops and sills. Built of finest *clear* fir, beautifully machined and finished.

Window Sash.—Of finest *clear* fir O. G. moulded, all edges and surfaces sanded and finished with great care.

Doors.—Inside doors, size 2 feet 8 inches by 6 feet 8 inches, carefully built of *clear* fir, all panels selected for attractive, velvety grain and beautifully finished on surfaces and edges. All doors mortised to receive lock sets. (See photographs, page 70.) All front doors of special design with glass in upper part. Double action door between kitchen and dining room.

Stairs.—Built from selected *clear* fir stock with especial attention to selection of grain. Newel post, moulded cap and base, circle tread, steps, risers, railing and balusters carefully finished. All parts of stairs are framed, housed and machined to fit and the whole is carefully boxed by itself to insure arrival in perfect condition.

Interior Woodwork.—Baseboard, base shoe door and window casing all selected *clear,* beautifully machined and ready to receive the oils, stains and varnishes. Casings are of molded and modern back band design.

Lock Sets.—Frosted brass. Front door sets have night latch and two-way knobs.

Hardware.—Window weights, sash lifts, hinges, nails of all proper sizes, glass, putty, tin flashing.

Paints.—The highest priced paint on the market is furnished for all Aladdin houses. It is manufactured of pure white lead, and color. Thirty-two colors to choose from. Your selections may follow your own tastes for body, trim, porch floor, sash, steps, etc. Send for color card.

Stains.—The *best* manufactured, are supplied for inside work. You may secure any effects you desire for interior decoration. Stain and varnish, or oil and varnish if you wish to finish in the natural wood, whichever you prefer. Lattice work under porch floors and shingle stain for roofs not included in prices.

Lath and Plaster.—You may have either lath and plaster or plaster board for inside walls, whichever you choose. Grounds are furnished where lath and plaster are supplied.

Outside Steps.—Steps of correct height and width for design of house. All cut to fit. Cellar stairs always included where shown on floor plan. All dimensions on floor plans are given outside to center for customers convenience. Send for foundation plan before starting your foundation.

All of which is covered by our *all inclusive guaranty.*

Industrial Housing Problems

A SPECIAL study of housing problems as related to industrial institutions has been made by the Aladdin organization. This study has been based on actual experience in building six new cities with Aladdin houses, and in furnishing groups of houses for many manufacturing concerns, mines in many localities and government projects.

We have handled almost every situation arising out of industrial housing necessities from a thirty-five room hotel furnished complete for operation; the building itself, heating, lighting, plumbing, furniture, stoves, dishes, silver, linen, carpets, rugs and decorations. We have on file, plans from which we have built dormitories, bunk houses, community dining halls, guard houses, bath houses, school houses, churches, offices and gymnasiums.

A cottage designed especially for a large project recently completed.

Our organization includes experienced landscape architects, engineers, construction superintendents, and all other factors for laying out, constructing and completing communities. See index page for pictures of Aladdin communities.

If interested, send for special information on this subject.

Aladdin House Plans in Perspective Drawings

Walk into the homes, inspect the living rooms, notice the placing of dining room furniture, then peep into the bedrooms of the Aladdin Homes shown on the following pages. Yes, even the kitchen shows an arrangement for efficiency.

This is the result of Aladdin's tirelesss efforts to bring complete information on Aladdin Homes to you, to make it possible for you to visit each Aladdin Home and mark its distinctive features, compare them and then select the home of your liking.

In a few instances, it was impossible to include perspective floor plans. However, they will be sent to you upon request.

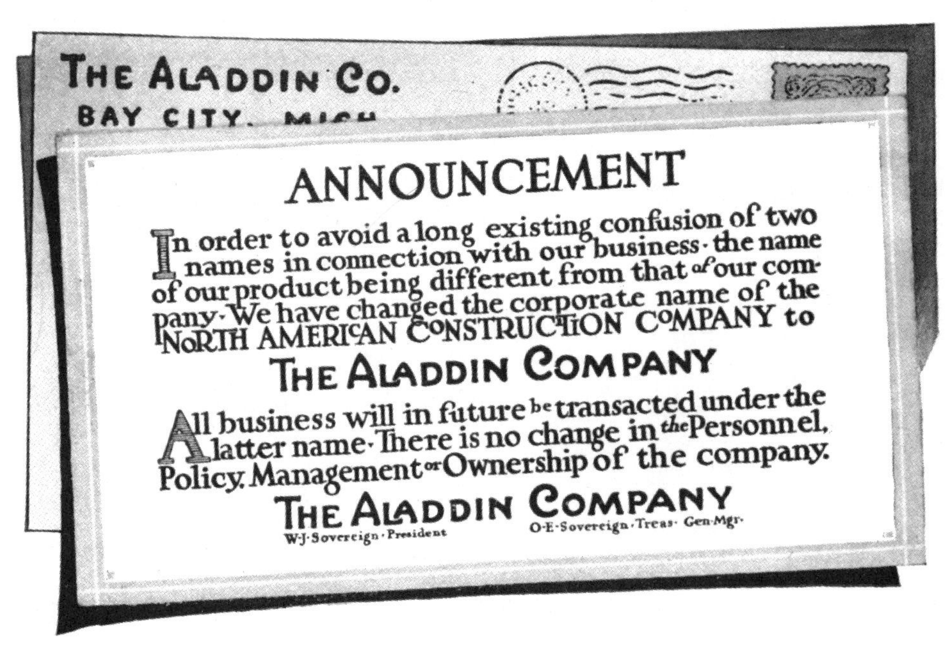

THE ALADDIN CO.
BAY CITY

ANNOUNCEMENT

In order to avoid a long existing confusion of two names in connection with our business - the name of our product being different from that of our company - We have changed the corporate name of the NORTH AMERICAN CONSTRUCTION COMPANY to

THE ALADDIN COMPANY

All business will in future be transacted under the latter name - There is no change in the Personnel, Policy, Management or Ownership of the company.

THE ALADDIN COMPANY

W-J-Sovereign - President O-E-Sovereign - Treas - Gen-Mgr-

The Raymond $585.20

Price, $616.00
Cash discount, 5%
Net price, $585.20

FOR compactness, convenience and modern designing, the Raymond is among the leaders. When entering the front through the attractively designed bungalow door, one is at once impressed with the roominess of this apparently small house. This long stretch of nearly 25 ft. is secured because of the wide arch separating the living and dining rooms. In this, as in all Aladdin houses, the designer has kept prominently in mind the thought of modern arrangements, which in Aladdins is only another way of saying, "doing one's work with the least possible effort." Notice how the kitchen, apparently in the remote part of the house, is conveniently accessible to the dining room and pantry. These "step-saving arrangements" are the things that help to make "doing one's own work" a real pleasure. What housewife would not be delighted with the plan of the Raymond? Of course, the exposed rafters, casement windows and porch all contribute their part to make this little bungalow complete, attractive and modern. If desired, siding can be substituted for wall shingles without extra cost.

Refer to page 70 and note the beautiful two panel door that is furnished for all Aladdin Houses. These doors are built of Fir and finish beautifully when stained natural or dark oak.

See Terms on page 2 and General Specifications on pages 12 and 13.

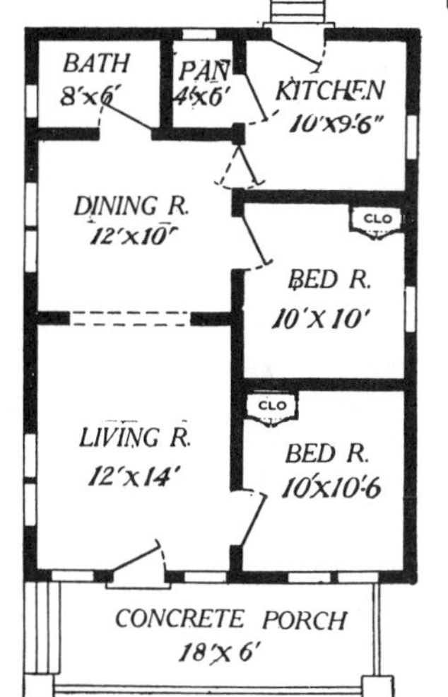

Floor Plan—The Raymond

An Autumn Day with The Maples

THE MAPLES is of the more conservative type of bungalow. At first glance, you will notice that simple lines are here made into a practical, substantial home. It has found great favor among Aladdin customers. The low roof, wide eaves, odd windows, exposed rafter ends and altogether attractive simplicity make a very pretty exterior without going to extremes in decoration. Much credit for the convenient arrangement of the interior is due to the fact that the house is square. Notice the manner in which the sleeping rooms occupying one side of the house are separated from the living rooms. The spacious living room

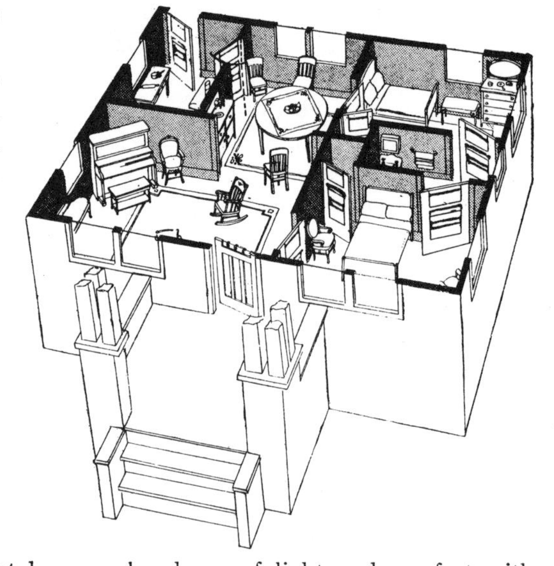

at the front has an abundance of light and comfort with outside entrance, entrance to front sleeping room and wide entrance to the dining room. Dining room is easily reached from back bedroom, living room and kitchen, and is well lighted on all sides. The kitchen is placed opposite dining room with outside entrance to the rear. Owners of the Maples claim for it the most convenient and comfortable arrangement. Ask us for names of Maples owners near you and let them tell you in their own words. See General Specifications, pages 12 and 13. Detail specifications for the Maples will be sent you on request. See Terms on page 2.

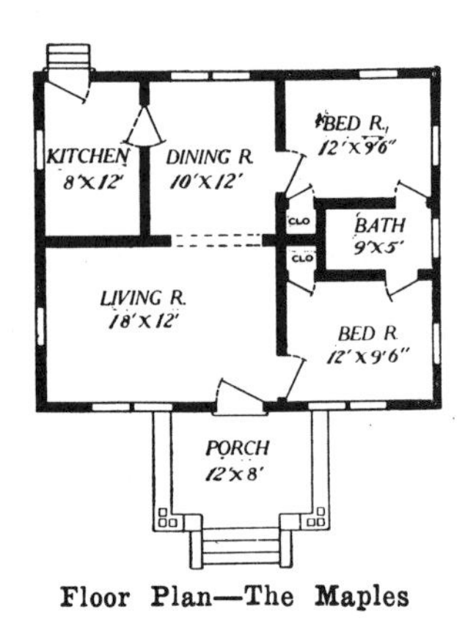

Floor Plan—The Maples

$726.75

Price, $765.00
Cash discount, 5%
Net price, $726.75

The Roseland $687.80

Price, $724.00
Cash discount, 5%
Net price, $687.80

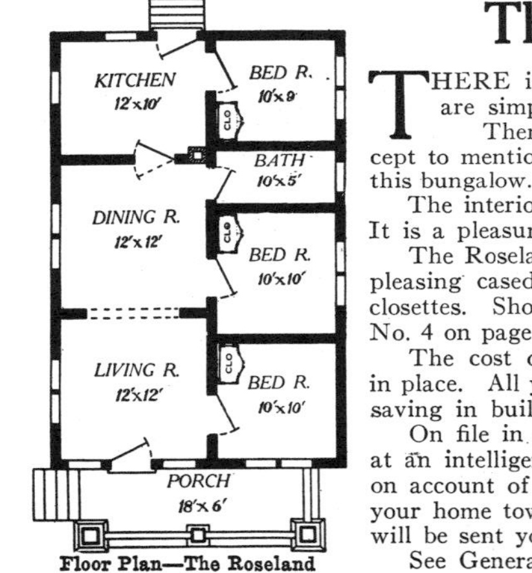

Floor Plan—The Roseland

THERE is something very restful and satisfying in this artistic bungalow. The structural lines throughout are simple without excess adornment and in this lies the secret of its distinction.

There is a roomy front porch with the pergola roof effect terminating at one end with the steps. Except to mention the simplicity of the structural lines it is quite impossible to intelligently define the popularity of this bungalow.

The interior of the house is planned so that the maximum of comfort may be had with the minimum of work. It is a pleasure to do housekeeping in this bungalow as it is easy to keep the rooms clean and sweet.

The Roseland contains seven rooms conveniently arranged. The living and dining rooms are connected by a pleasing cased archway (see Interior Illustration, page 45). Each of the three bedrooms are furnished with closettes. Should you intend to put a basement under the bungalow we would recommend using our addition No. 4 on page 108 of our catalog.

The cost of erecting the Roseland is small. When you receive the material it is all cut-to-fit ready to nail in place. All your carpenters do is the erecting—no sawing, no measuring, no cutting to fit. Besides, think of the saving in building an Aladdin—no waste material to pay for.

On file in our offices we have plans as basis for estimating costs. With this plan you will be able to arrive at an intelligent price for the complete home. It is impossible to give a fixed cost of erection for all localities on account of difference in cost of labor, etc. Hence you are able to find the cost of the Roseland erected in your home town by applying local figures and using the tables shown on the Aladdin estimate sheets. A copy will be sent you upon request.

See General Specifications on pages 12 and 13. See Terms on page 2.

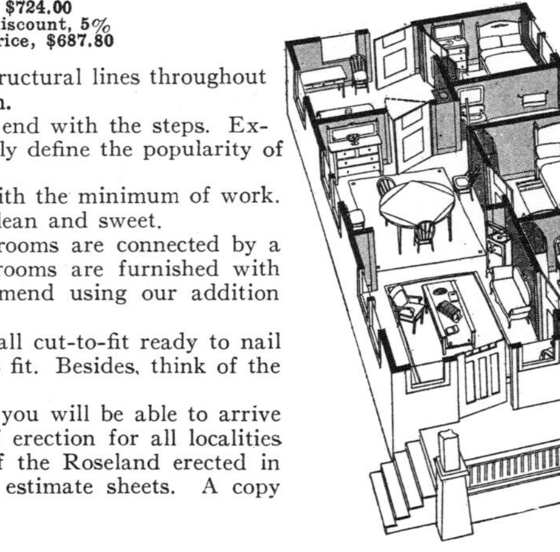

The Wilmont
$1,064.00

Price, $1,120.00
Cash discount, 5%
Net price, $1,064.00

"WHAT a well designed and attractive home," were the words of an out-of-town visitor who recently inspected one of our "Wilmont" bungalows erected in Bay City.

This same expression has been repeated many times by our local people. As you cannot make this personal inspection, we have endeavored to give you a true reproduction of this home in all its beauty.

You can see by looking at the photograph that this house is made particularly pleasing to the eye because it is so well proportioned. The eaves on the front and rear gables are supported by heavy brackets with exposed rafters at the sides and the wide belt in front and back and double shingled courses are also other distinctive marks. The main roof is balanced by two attractive dormers one on each side.

The offset front porch broadens the apparent size of the house. Handsome square tapered columns support a gable roof, the porch roof harmonizing in every detail with the main roof.

Summer breezes will always find some portion of the porch exposed and the summer sun will always find some part protected.

Many beautiful color schemes for the exterior are possible, and our Department of Service has on file many attractive color schemes and suggestions that will be sent to you on request.

The interior arrangement of the "Wilmont" is modern in every respect and can be attractively finished and furnished (see Interior Illustrations, page 45). The living room extends across the entire front of the house; the size—20 feet wide by 12 feet deep—offers many opportunities for attractive arrangement of furniture. A semi-open stairway leading to the second floor adds another touch of beauty to the appearance of the living room. The dining room is large and well planned. Good wall space is provided on two sides, while the two windows add a flood of light by day. The wide cased arch which separates the living room from the dining room is a pleasant feature in connection with this plan.

PORCH 12'x5'
KITCHEN 8'x11'8"
DINING R. 12'x13'
PANT.
LIVING R. 20'x12'
PORCH 14'x6'

First Floor Plan
The Wilmont

CLO.
BED R. 10'x12'
BED R. 10'x12
HALL
BATH 8'x6'
CLOS. 8'x2'8"
BED R. 16'6"x12'
CLOS.
ROOF

Second Floor Plan
The Wilmont

Three large bedrooms on the second floor with bath and closets complete the upstair plan. The bedrooms have a maximum height of 8 ft. ceilings with slightly sloping ceilings to the side walls. These sloping ceilings do not interfere with head room or the placing of furniture, and make the bedrooms cosy in appearance. See terms on page 2 and general specifications on pages 12 and 13.

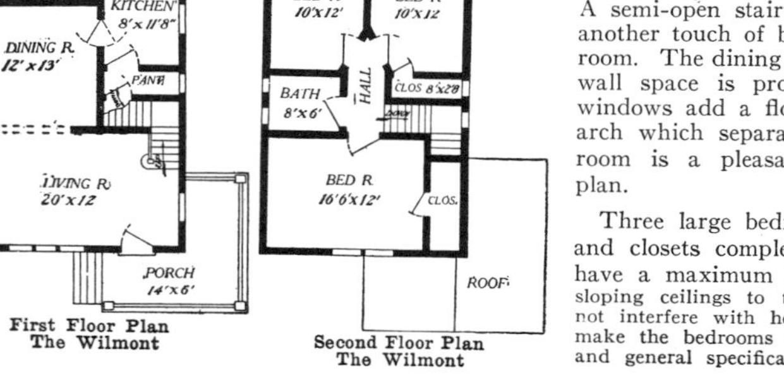

The Carolina $1,140.00

Price, $1,200.00
Cash discount, 5%
Net price, $1,140.00

HERE is a strong, substantial-looking home that impresses everyone. It has some exceptionally desirable advantages not found in any other design. In the first place, the price we have been able to place on it is truly astonishing for its conveniences. Four good bedrooms—think of it! One bedroom is downstairs. Every bedroom has a good closet, with an especially large extra closet in the front bedroom. Two grouped windows flood the living room with light and air. Wide arch separates the dining room and living room, giving a 26-foot vista across the house. The massive roof with heavy grouped columns on porch gives a very substantial appearance. This house is certainly a credit to any owner.

See Terms on page 2 and General Specifications on pages 12 and 13.

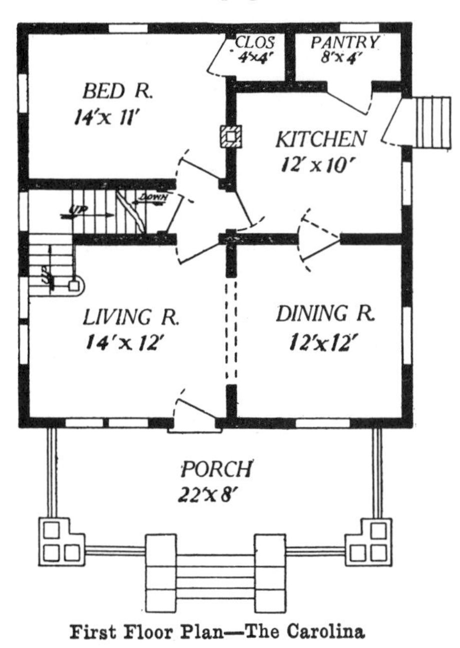

First Floor Plan—The Carolina

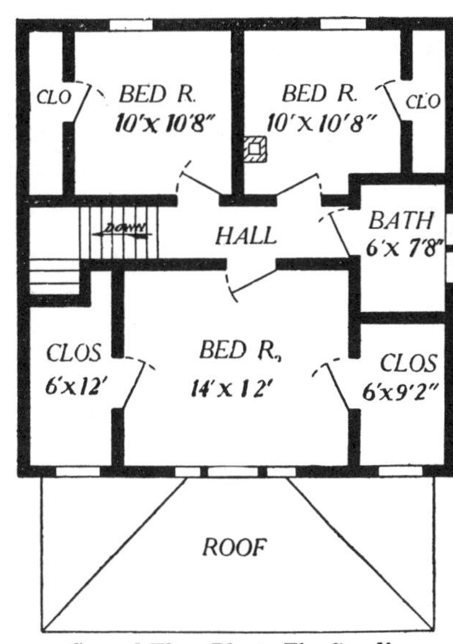

Second Floor Plan—The Carolina

The Lamberton $1,995.00

Price, $2,100.00
Cash discount, 5%
Net price, $1,995.00

THIS striking design has many delightfully original ideas. The pleasing proportion of its generous roof and the heavy timbered effects under eaves and windows, give stability and strength to the general impression. Study the hooded front entrance supported by heavy brackets. A pergola type of porch covering just fits in the right way. Also note the heavy abutment-like porch piers. The exterior is rough cast stucco but is sometimes furnished with shingled walls, the shingles to be stained a pearl gray, or left to weather.

The Lamberton is a genuine American home. Its lines are American—straight, simple and massive.

Exterior trim seems to be confined to small divided lights in windows with heavy false window sills supported by brackets.

The brackets on the eaves are simple, and especially designed for this home.

Notice the front entrance—a particular feature of this home. The front door has practically a full length glass which is divided in keeping with the general idea in the windows. The sidelights on each side of the front door are built to harmonize.

And what a splendid arrangement of

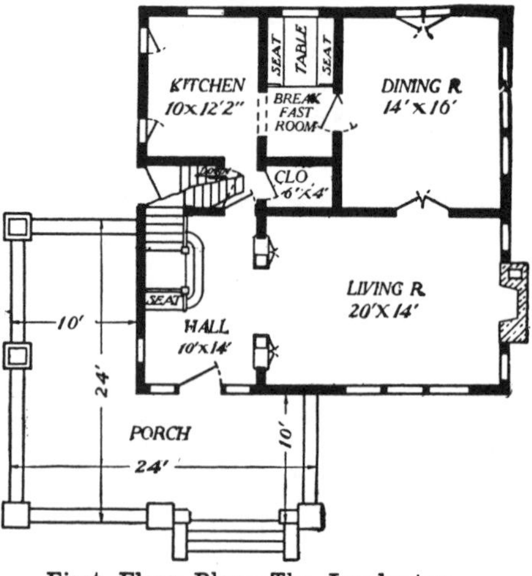

First Floor Plan—The Lamberton

Fireplace with Bookcases—The Lamberton

Living Room, Reception Hall and Staircase
The Lamberton

rooms. The reception hall is separated from living room by a wide columned arch with bookcases built in.

The handsome staircase presents a very attractive appearance as you will note by referring to plan that a seat is arranged in front of the lower landing, the stairs being turned at the landing toward the living room.

The reception hall is well lighted. The front door and sidelights with small casement window at the side give an even light to hall and stairway.

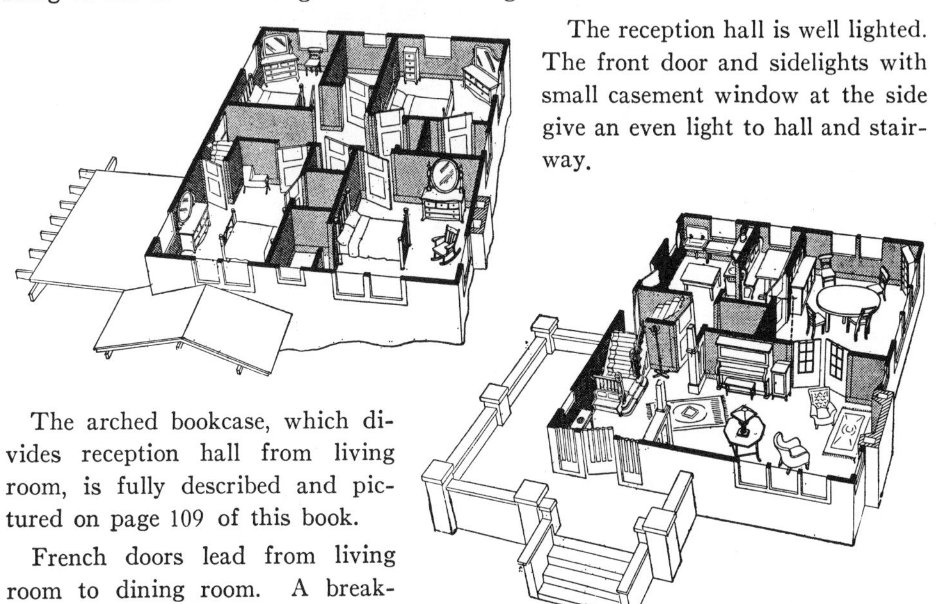

The arched bookcase, which divides reception hall from living room, is fully described and pictured on page 109 of this book.

French doors lead from living room to dining room. A breakfast room separates dining room and kitchen. Entrance to kitchen is from either breakfast room, grade entrance or reception hall. A large cloak closet is conveniently placed. The second floor has four good, light, airy bedrooms, closets and bath. The third floor gives an attic thirty by thirty feet.

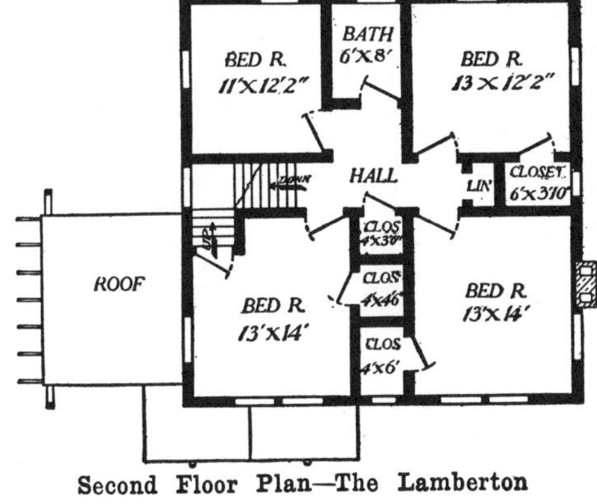

Second Floor Plan—The Lamberton

The bookcases shown in the illustration with fireplace on this page are not included with the Lamberton at the price quoted. Should you desire to include them in your home you will find them described on page 111.

Could more conveniences be offered in any home of its size than are incorporated in the Lamberton?

See Terms on page 2 and General Specifications on pages 12 and 13.

The Kentucky

The Kentucky $1,282.50

Price, No. 1, $1,350.00
Cash discount, 5%
Net price, $1,282.50

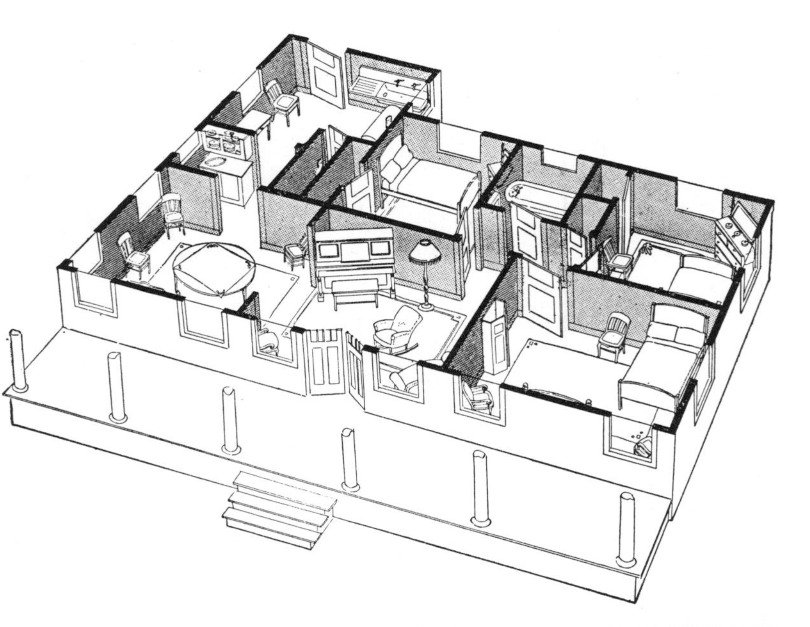

IS it not a beauty in every line? Simplicity is the keynote, yet what could be added to improve its attractions? While it reminds one of the stately colonnades of old Colonial mansions, it still retains the delightful atmosphere of modern American bungalows. The broad expanse of porch, with plain Tuscan columns and projecting eaves successfully blends these two most desirable types without losing the dignity of the one nor the cosy homeiness of the other. Double front doors seem to open wide a hospitality of true American spirit. Casement windows with divided lights swing into living room, dining room, and bedroom from the porch. Both living room and dining room are unusually well lighted. The Kentucky Bungalow has made a remarkable impression on our customers, having attained as great a degree of popularity as any design we have ever produced. You will be interested in the Interior Illustrations of the Kentucky shown on page 79 of this book. The two views shown—living room and dining room—give a fair idea of the large amount of space provided for furniture arrangements. The owner of the Kentucky from which these interior views were made included a built-in buffet in the dining room. The living room is very large and surely presents an inviting appearance. The Department of Service has many excellent suggestions on file for interior decoration of the Kentucky. We will be glad to send you suggestions upon request or work out the details of your ideas if you will send them to us. The window blinds shown are included with the Kentucky. Study General Specifications, pages 12 and 13. Exact detail specifications of the Kentucky will be sent upon request, which will enable you to make careful estimate on cost of erection. See Terms on page 2.

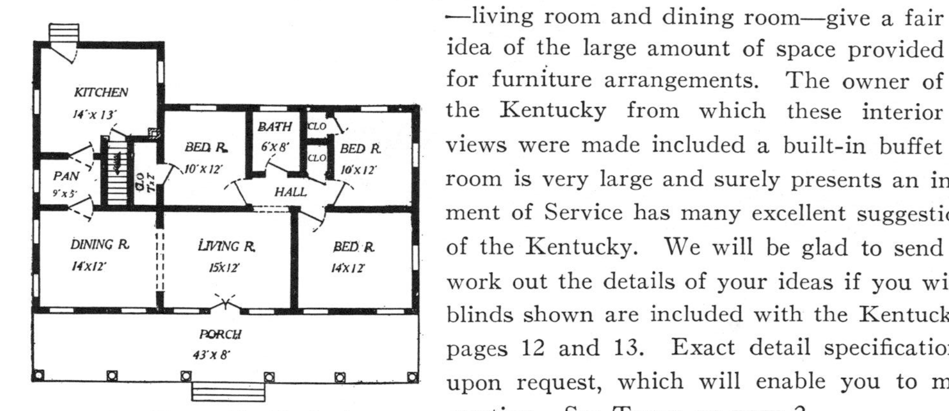

Floor Plan The Kentucky

A Porch Designed for Summer Comfort—Wide, Open and Attractive

First Floor Plan—The Villa

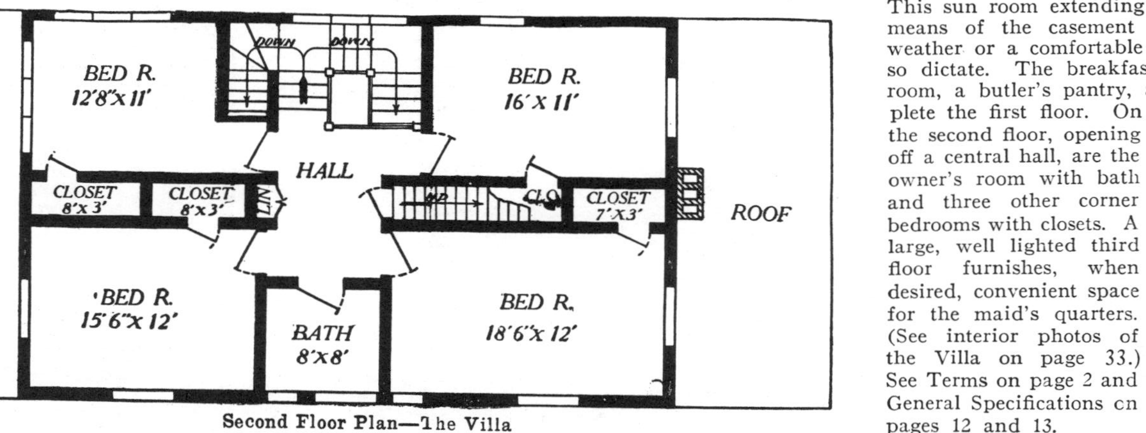

Second Floor Plan—The Villa

The Villa $3,420.00

Price, $3,600.00
Cash discount, 5%
Net price, $3,420.00

IT is difficult to select words suitable to describe the beauties and convenience of this thoroughly modern home. While the architectural lines are strong, yet the artist has rendered them extremely pleasing to the eye. The pergola effect at the front and each side, combined with the stately columns, lends a certain dignity and grandeur that at once places The Villa in a class by itself. Like the beautiful everywhere, this house challenges the lover of the artistic and furnishes a concrete example of stateliness and strength which at the same time is an embodiment of the finest culture.

On passing through the vestibuled front entrance into the large and spacious hallway, the visitor's attention is at once attracted by the beautiful and easily ascending stairs at the rear, and on each side by the double French doors leading either to the living room on the right or the large dining room on the left. Without changing one's position, there is easily visible across the living room the French doors leading to the sun parlor. This sun room extending the entire width of the house, affords by means of the casement windows a protected porch in pleasant weather or a comfortable lounging room when the elements outside so dictate. The breakfast room, ample for a small family dining room, a butler's pantry, and a conveniently arranged kitchen complete the first floor. On the second floor, opening off a central hall, are the owner's room with bath and three other corner bedrooms with closets. A large, well lighted third floor furnishes, when desired, convenient space for the maid's quarters. (See interior photos of the Villa on page 33.) See Terms on page 2 and General Specifications cn pages 12 and 13.

The Dresden $817.00

Price, $860.00
Cash discount, 5%
Net price, $817.00

THE DRESDEN will appeal to you as being an ideal home. The picture, which was taken on a midsummer's day, shows a number of features that are not found in the average home. Notice the porch—the shelter and relief it provides from the hot summer sun. Every inch of the one hundred and twenty square feet of floor space on this porch seems to hold a charm for the comfort seeker. And as much can be said of the inside of the home. Notice the picture, showing windows raised. It is possible to practically open up the home on four sides giving the utmost in ventilation. making all rooms light and airy, cool and pleasant.

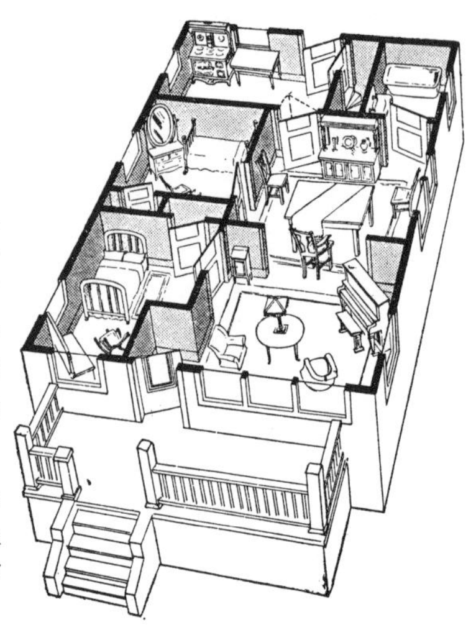

Before reading further, look over the floor plan carefully. What do you think of it? Isn't it just right for convenience—doesn't it appeal to your ideas of "home?" Notice the long stretch—practically twenty-four feet—thru living room and dining room. Now inspect the interior photographs of the Dresden shown on this page.

The three views shown give you an idea of the attractiveness of this exceptional home. Can you wonder why hundreds of builders over the country have selected it for their home?

INTERIOR VIEW-THE DRESDEN-"JUST AS YOU STEP IN THE FRONT DOOR"

DINING ROOM, THE DRESDEN

LIVING ROOM, THE DRESDEN

The interior photograph at the top was taken from the front entrance. It shows a portion of the living room, the cased arch which separates the dining room shown to the left of the picture. At the bottom of the page views of the living room and dining room are shown.

KITCHEN 15'x 8'
BATH 6'x8'
BED R. 10'x 10'
DINING R. 14'x12'
CLOS CLOS
BED R. 10'x 12'
LIVING R. 14'x12'
PORCH 20'x8'

Floor Plan—The Dresden

The daylight rooms are arranged on one side of the home and possess every desired feature—plenty of light and air, spaciousness and ease in accessibility; adapted to any arrangement or setting of furniture. Plenty of space in the bedrooms with good closets in each, makes a home that will give you great satisfaction and much convenience. Your friends will agree with your judgment in selecting this home of homes—the Dresden. All of the pictures shown in the Aladdin catalog are from photographs sent us of actual Aladdin homes erected in different parts of the country by our customers. This is true of practically no other catalog. The photographs show what you can do with Aladdin's Readi-Cut System of Construction and Aladdin's Dollar-A-Knot lumber. See General Specifications, pages 12 and 13. Detail specifications for the Dresden will be sent on request. See Terms on page 2.

Exclusive Aladdin Advantages

Originators of the Readi-Cut System of Construction; Eight years longer in the business than any other concern; Dollar-A-Knot Guaranty; Highest Award at World's Fair; Customers in almost every community in the Country; Indorsed by Uncle Sam.

The Yale $934.80

Price, $984.00
Cash discount, 5%
Net price, $934.80

THE full realization of a complete home is gratified in the Yale. The judgment of Aladdin designers has been wonderfully approved in the hundreds of sales of this design. When you fully comprehend all that it offers, you will be as enthusiastic about it as every customer who is living in it.

First Floor Plan The Yale

Second Floor Plan The Yale

Harmony of design and proportion first strikes the eye. With a width of twenty feet, making it adaptable to narrow lots, it accomplished a two-story plan without its height being apparent. Four gables afford a surprising amount of room in the second story. Concrete pedestals support square porch columns and the long balusters of the porch railing are different from the usual type. A beautiful front door leads into the living room which extends full width of the house. Arched opening separates living room from dining room. Kitchen, cellar way and rear porch complete the first story. On the second story are found the bedrooms, bath and closet. You will be delighted by the selection of the Yale and especially the surpassing beauty of the interior woodwork which lends itself to the most interesting decorative schemes. Our Wood Stains, and varnish permit your taste to be realized to the fullest extent. See General Specifications on pages 12 and 13. Complete detail specifications for the Yale will be sent on request. See Terms on page 2.

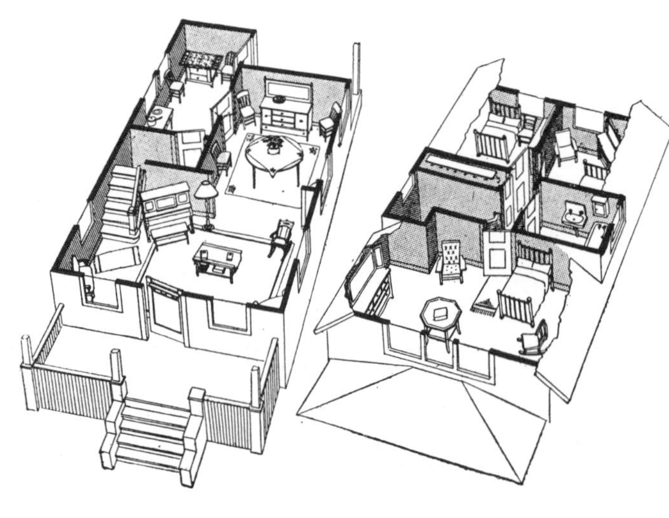

The Plaza $1,499.10

Price, $1,578.00
Cash discount, 5%
Net price, $1,499.10

THIS magnificent bungalow secures inspiration from one of the best known bungalows in Pasadena, California. An interesting effect is secured by the treatment of gables composing the roof. This is highly typical of the true California bungalow. To the lover of large porches the Plaza has an especially strong appeal. The front section of porch extends twenty-six feet from the entrance to the left, and thirty-one feet from the front along the side. Over the rear section of the side porch a timbered pergola gives opportunity for vines. Entering the front door you have a view through the living room and dining room for thirty feet. Just off the dining room, and with direct entrance to the kitchen, is a dainty breakfast room. This room can, of course, be used as a den or sewing room, at the owner's discretion. Grade cellar entrance from the kitchen, three fine bedrooms, bath and closets complete this splendid floor plan arrangement. A true craftsman front door, and our famous Arch A-1 illustrated in back of catalog are included in the price. This arch may be used as bookcases, facing the living room, or china closets facing the dining room. Owners of the Plaza are delighted with it, as you cannot fail to be should you select it. It will save you from $400 to $900 under what could be built by the old way of building, with inferior materials. Send for complete detail specifications. See General Specifications, page 12 and 13.

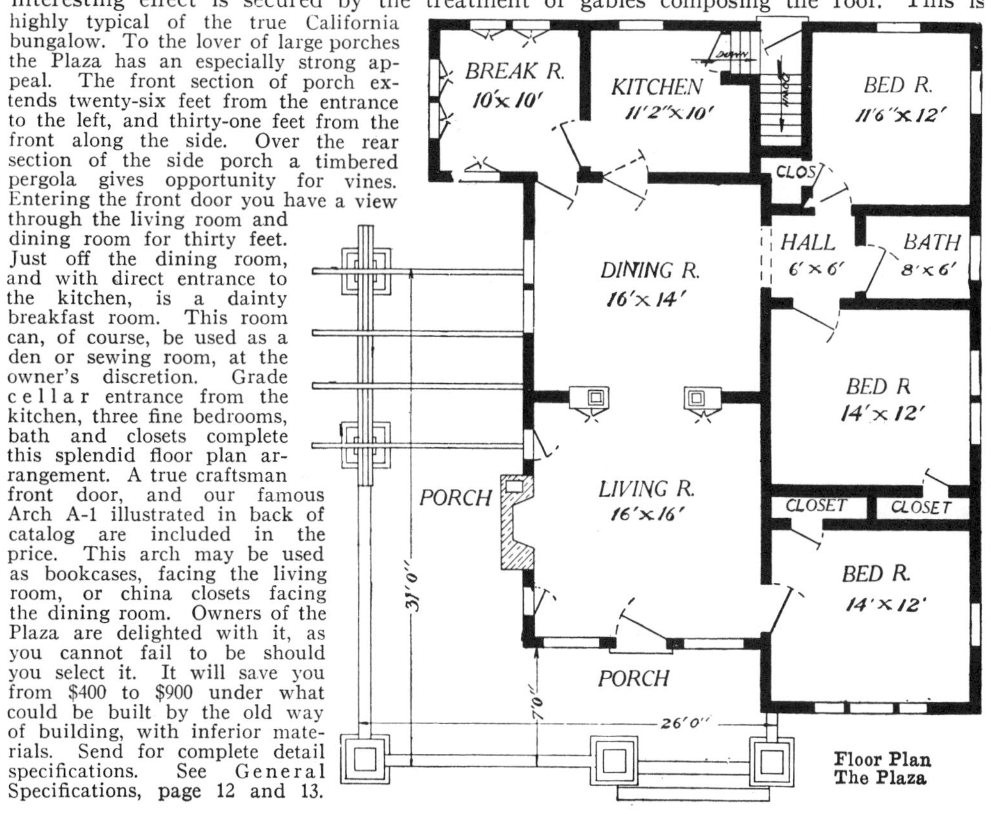

Floor Plan The Plaza

The Colonial $1,898.10

Price, $1,998.00
Cash discount, 5%
Net price, $1,898.10

THIS modern home with its distinctive features has a large number of admirers. The general appearance, both design and arrangement of detail, place it in a class of its own. The general lines are taken from New England and Southern Colonial architecture, while many original ideas are added.

The windows, with divided lights and simple dormers breaking the front roof, are purely of New England origin, and are often referred to as "severe, simple and quiet."

Credit is due Southern designers for the semicircle porch and front entrance detail. By close inspection you will notice that the heavy front door is balanced on either side by sidelights. The detail in both door and

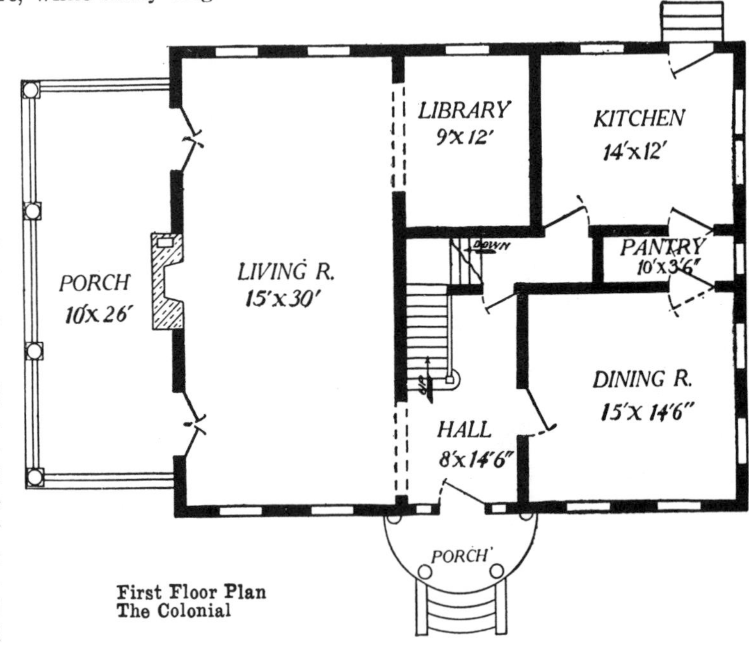

First Floor Plan
The Colonial

side-lights harmonize, as both have glass in upper hall. Besides the decorative value of this feature it is practical in that it provides a flood of light in the reception hall, lighting stairs and passageways. The semi-circle porch with balcony effect is supported by four large turned columns.

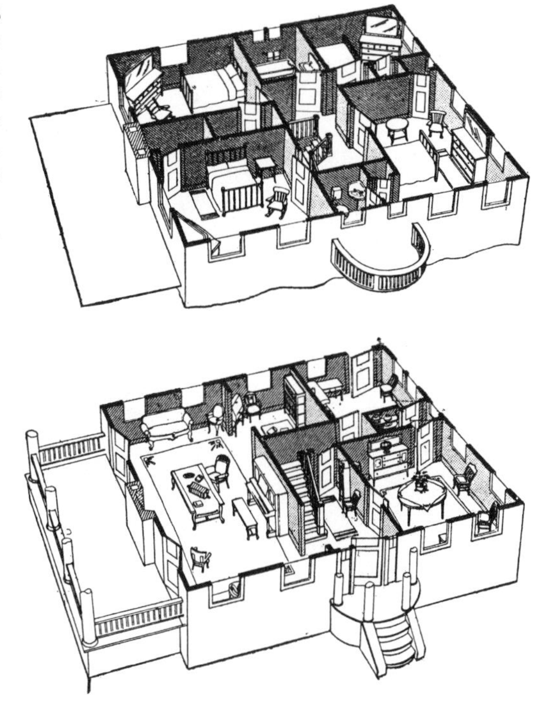

The broad and spacious side porch is also of interest. It is one of the most typical features of Colonial architecture. The balusters and rail are extended around the porch, entrance to be had from the two doors in the living room on either side of the fireplace or from the steps at the side.

The Colonial is shown here with terrace breaking abruptly a short distance from the front. This is another Southern feature that is proving very popular among builders of better class homes today.

The interior expresses modern ideas. The large size porch is an excellent summer season auxiliary to the living room, as both run parallel, with entrance doors on either side of the fireplace. The living room is arranged at one end of the home. The size, 15 feet wide by 30 feet long, offers many opportunities for different and tasty arrangements of furniture. The fireplace which is shown in the plan adds much to the comfort and attractiveness of the room and is well located. The library which directly adjoins living room has excellent wall space for book-cases and library furniture. The location of this room makes it suitable for either library or den. The arrangement of dining room and kitchen is ideal. The dining room at the front right corner and kitchen at the rear are divided by butler's pantry.

The kitchen in this design has received considerable thought. Notice that you are able to reach front entrance through the hall to reception hall without passing through the other rooms. Double action doors prove convenient between kitchen and dining room. From the reception hall you can pass directly into the living room or dining room or into the kitchen. Four corner bedrooms on second floor are well ventilated and easily accessible to hallway and bathroom. This home is fascinating in appearance and has much of the sought-for distinction. Of course you will want to know a great many things about the Colonial, if this handsome home appeals to you; things that there is not enough space to tell about here. Upon request we will send complete detail specifications and go into all the interesting facts. Write us about your ideas. See General Specifications on pages 12 and 13. See Terms on page 2.

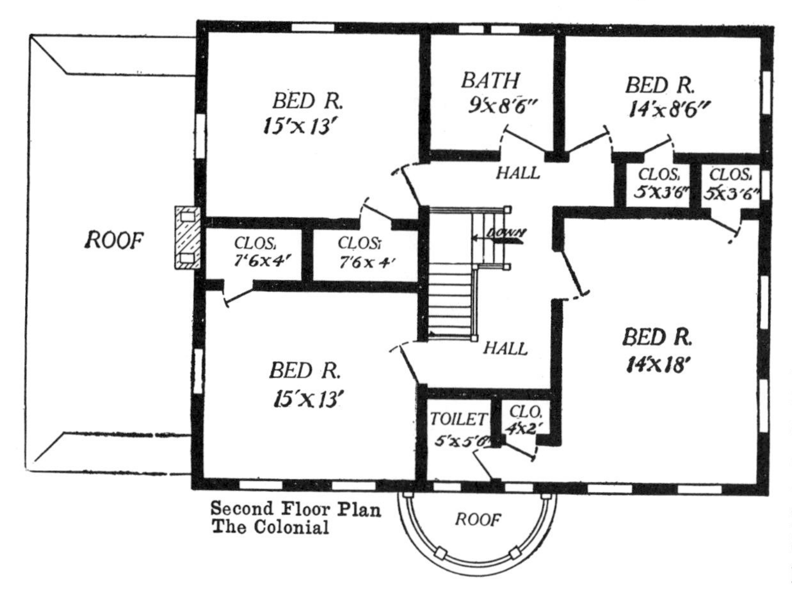

**Second Floor Plan
The Colonial**

The Herford

$836.00

Price, $880.00
Cash discount, 5%
Net price, $836.00

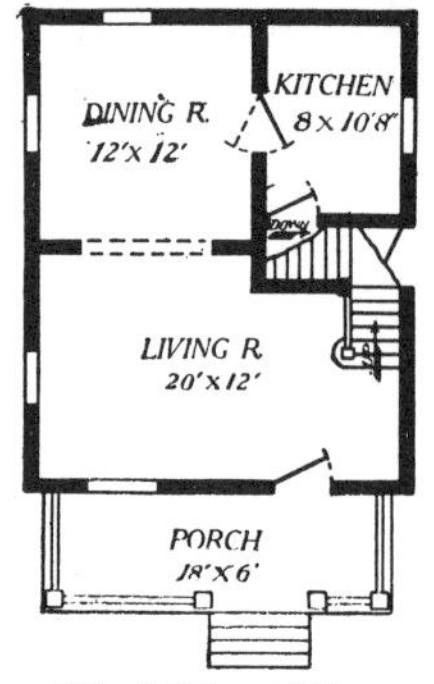

First Floor Plan
The Herford

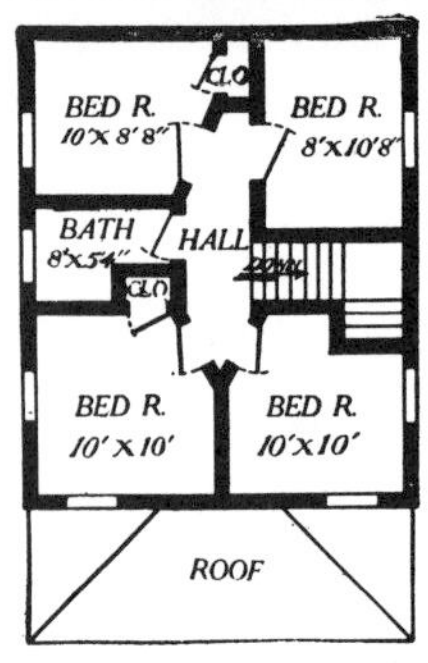

Second Floor Plan
The Herford

THE Herford is an achievement in building a two-story, four-bedroom house at a price less than nine hundred dollars, yet the convenience and attractive appearance of this design is not impaired in the least. A large living room across the entire front, large square dining room and kitchen make an exceptionally convenient and roomy first floor plan. The second floor has four bedrooms and bath, with clothes closets. The large porch across the front and the grade cellar entrance, are features of this design seldom found in a house at this price. Handsome front door with three-quarter length glass and wide window front the house. You couldn't possibly better the design and arrangement of the Herford, try as you might and it would be utterly impossible to find better lumber than is furnished, for it doesn't grow in any forest.

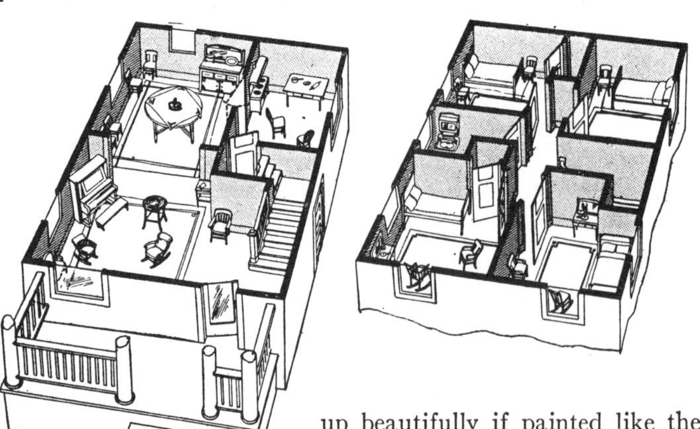

The carefully built semi-open stairway with circle first step, newel post and beautifully grained Fir lumber add a pleasing tone to the interior woodwork. All woodwork is very carefully sanded and ready to receive the stains and varnish. The Herford would show up beautifully if painted like the Charleston, which is shown in colors on another page.

See Terms on page 2 and General Specifications on pages 12 and 13.

Living Room-The Villa
Dining Room-The Villa
Sun Porch-The Villa

The Suburban

$1,075.40

Price, $1,132.00
Cash discount, 5%
Net price, $1,075.40

THE Suburban is well named, because how attractively this modern home will adorn the most desirable lot in the residential part of any of our progressive cities! Simple in construction, yet it is thoroughly modern in every line. Exposed scrolled rafters, cornice brackets, divided lights in the upper sash, attractive front door, combined with a suitable grouping of different style and sized windows furnish the distinguishing features in exterior design. The shingled gable tends to remove the plain appearance so often found in this style of house. The large living room, 24x12 feet, with semi-open stairs, a well lighted dining room separated from living room with wide archway; and convenient kitchen reached from dining room by a double action door make up the living apartments of the Suburban. Ascending the semi-open stairs, one reaches a central hall on second floor. No floor space has been wasted by our architect here as can be easily seen by noting the convenient bath and four large sized sleeping rooms, each one of which has a large clothes closet in connection. And please note that the lowest points in the bedrooms on the second floor of the Suburban are six feet in height.

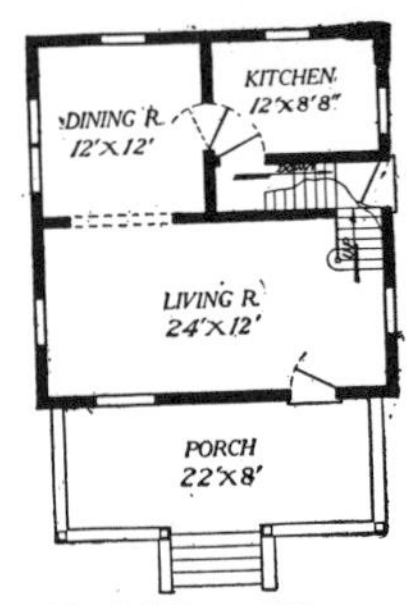

First Floor Plan
The Suburban

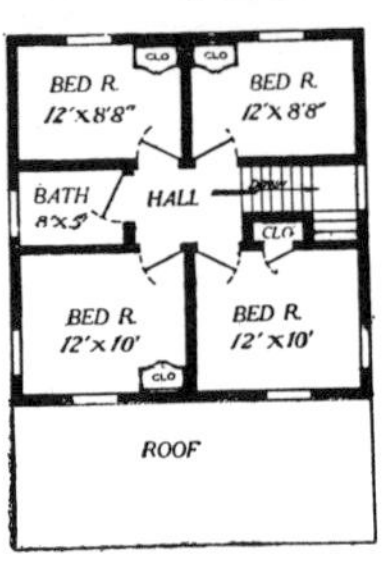

Second Floor Plan
The Suburban

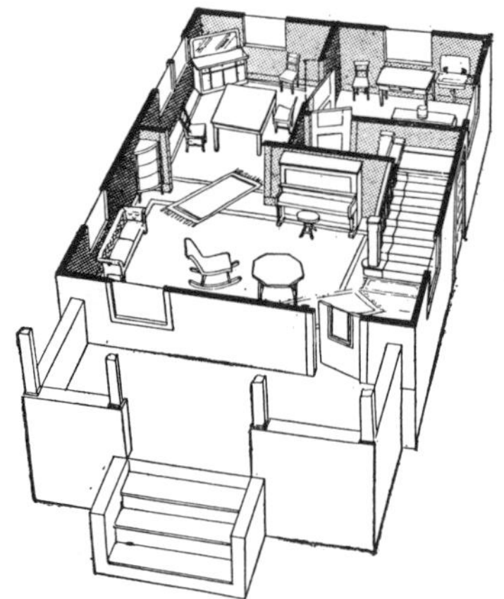

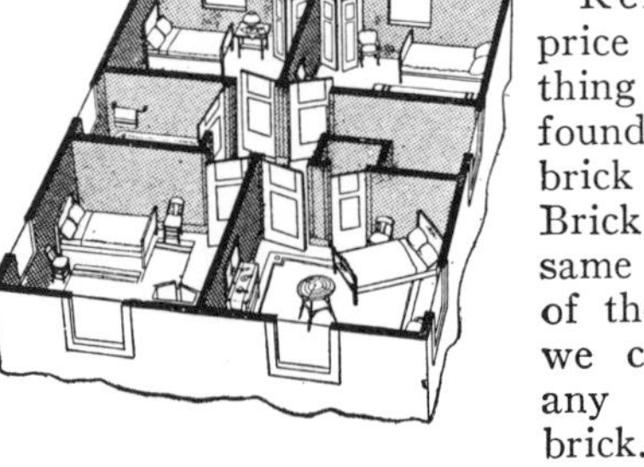

Remember our price includes everything above the foundation except the brick for the chimney. Brick costs about the same in every section of the country, hence we cannot save you any money on the brick. We can save every builder of a Suburban several hundred dollars.

See Terms on page 2 and General Specifications on pages 12 and 13.

The Rodney—A Comfortable Little Home

$1 A Knot Lumber

$340.10

Price, No. 1, $358.00
Cash discount, 5%
Net price, $340.10

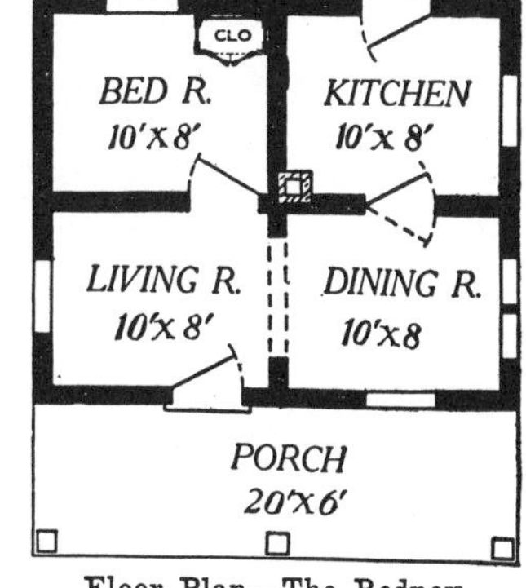

Floor Plan—The Rodney

MANY good American families are living happily and comfortably in Rodneys. Its four cosy rooms are all well arranged and its generous porch serves in a delightful way the outdoor pleasures of summer. A handsome front door with glass in upper part and embellished with mouldings would suitably fit a more costly home. The double casement window in the dining room, with English sash made to swing in appeals strongly to the housewife. All upper sash are divided into small lights.

You have your choice of two sizes in the Rodney. No. 1 is 20x22 feet over all and has four 10x8 foot rooms. Price given above. No. 2 is 24x26 feet and has four 10x12 foot rooms. Price, $426.00, cash discount 5%. Net price, $404.70. In both designs a wide arch separates the living room from the dining room. You will be delighted should you decide to own this cottage.

Of course, you receive our famous Dollar-A-Knot siding and all the materials entering the construction are positively the highest grades found anywhere. Frosted brass oak leaf design lock sets set off the beautifully grained doors and woodwork. In fact, you will have as finely finished a home as anyone. Two men can erect this house in four days. Most owners of the Rodney did all the work themselves, easily.

See Terms on page 2 and General Specifications on pages 12 and 13.

I am very proud of my bungalow and want to say that I received much better material than I could have bought here. It is admired by all. You may be sure when I build again you will get the order, for I saved nearly $600 on this deal.

—S. R. Bartlett.

The Sheffield $1,482.00

Price, $1,560.00
Cash discount, 5%
Net price, $1,482.00

DO not the roof and porch lines of the Sheffield please you? The heavy overhang and Japanese roof effect give an individuality to this attractive home that invariably pleases its owner. Notice the heavy porch columns and exposed scrolled rafters. How well these carry out the general architectural lines.

Ascending to the porch by the wide front steps, one is surprised with the size of the porch, 26x8 feet. An attractive front door and a French door lead into and through the vestibule to the living room. Notice the size, 26x15 feet, and the wide archway leading to the well lighted dining room. Arch A-1, page 109, is furnished for this archway. A kitchen with pantry and stairs leading to basement and grade entrance complete the first floor. From the living room our easily ascending semi-open stairs lead to a central hall on second floor. Opening off the hallway are three bedrooms and a bath.

While this picture of the Sheffield shows the side walls with the double shingled effect, yet when desired siding wthout extra cost will be substituted for shingles.

For a substantial, convenient, attractive home, don't you think the Sheffield is one of the best? See Terms on page 2 and General Specifications on pages 12 and 13.

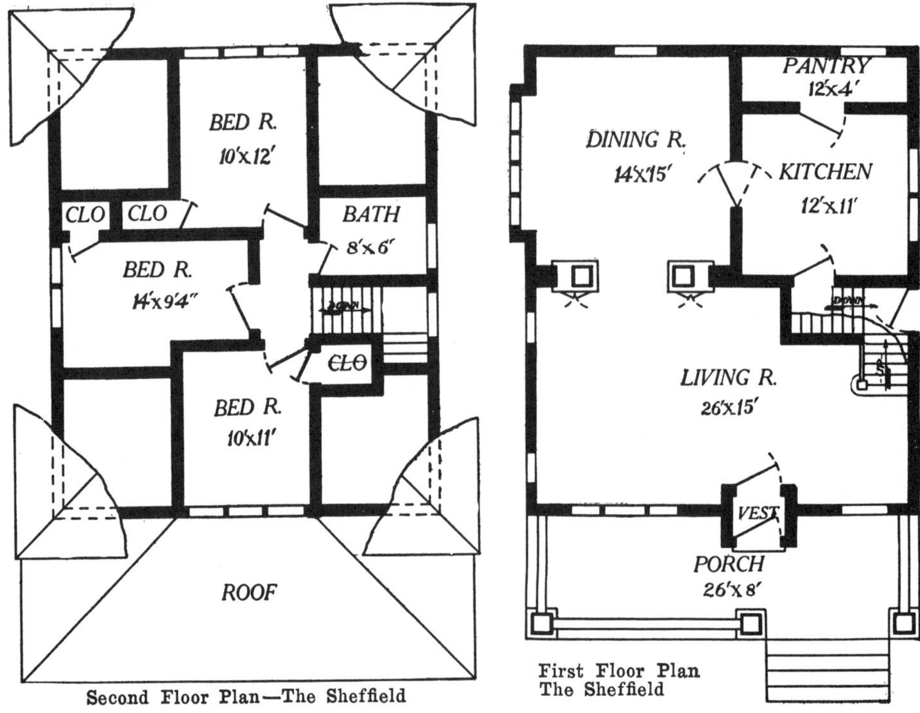

Second Floor Plan—The Sheffield

First Floor Plan
The Sheffield

The Rochester $1,387.00

Price, $1,460.00
Cash discount, 5%
Net price, $1,387.00

THE Rochester is of the strong, substantial American type. Square lines give the advantage of utilizing every inch of space to good advantage, while this particular house incorporates some features distinctive to itself. Note the vestibule, large living room with cosy bedroom having projecting bay window; group window in dining room; large pantry attached to kitchen and rear exit grade cellar entrance. Three bedrooms, sewing room, bath and closets complete the second story. Most of the windows are grouped in pairs. Scrolled rafter ends embellish the eaves. Taken altogether, the Rochester is a most satisfying home. On a one-thousand-dollar lot the Rochester would normally sell for at least $5,500. You can easily comprehend the profit available to the owner should conditions arise that he would want to sell it. Owners of Aladdin houses find that the high quality of finish, material, both inside and outside helps make quick sales when a sale is desired.

The Rochester was first built up in Northern Minnesota and the owner is high in his praise of the warmth of Aladdin construction.

See Terms on page 2 and General Specifications on pages 12 and 13.

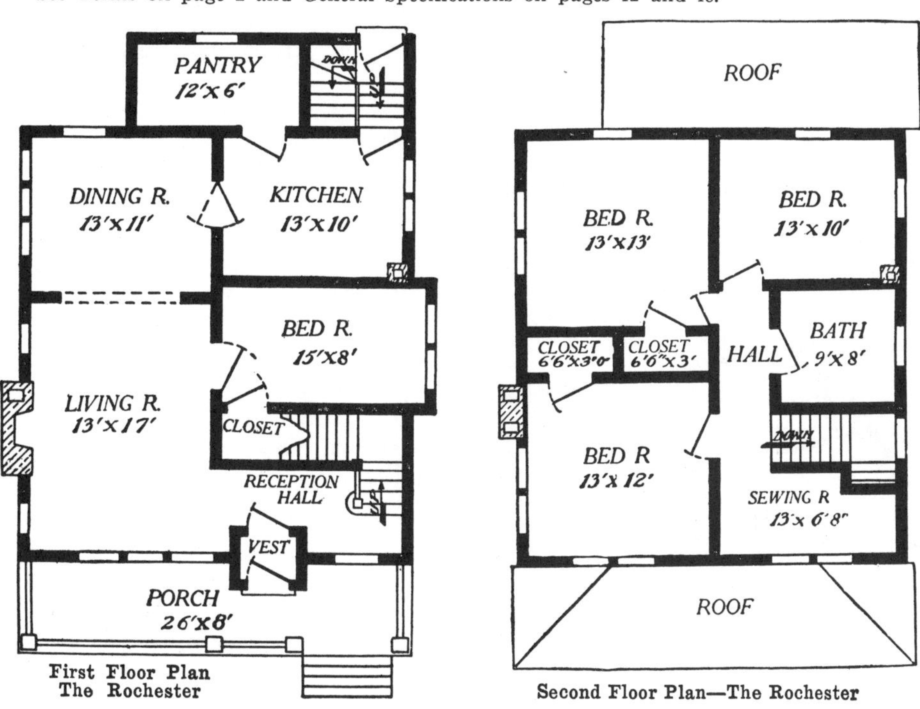

First Floor Plan
The Rochester

Second Floor Plan—The Rochester

The Castle $518.70

Price, $546.00
Cash discount, 5%
Net price, $518.70

WHERE have you seen a home that was better adapted to a corner lot or a lot between streets than the Castle? Notice the living room and dining room. Both are located at the front of the house, and both are separated from the kitchen, with no inconvenience to the housewife. But now, notice the price. Have you ever heard of a like bargain? It is hard to realize that this home can be purchased at this low figure. Think of it, complete material at a price that would not ordinarily buy a three-room house at the local lumber dealers. In addition to your getting this home at one-half the usual cost, you get a better home.

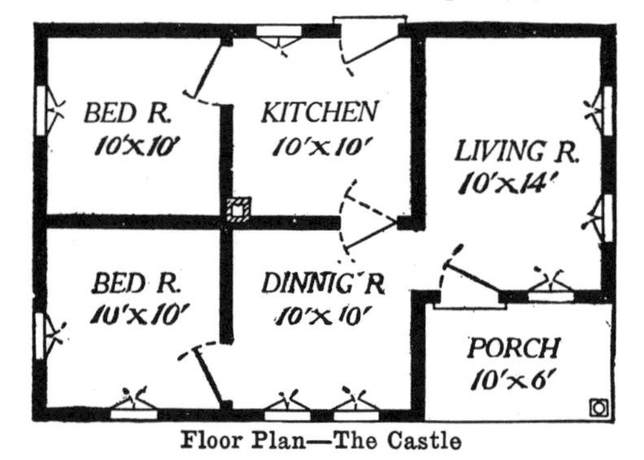

Floor Plan—The Castle

The Aladdin Readi-Cut System of Home Building is better than the old saw-measure-fit-on-the-ground system because it accomplishes the work *better, quicker,* and *cheaper.* Every piece of material in the house—siding, flooring, studding, joists, rafters, etc., is cut-to-fit in our mills by the finest machines. The result is accuracy of joints, and your house is stronger, warmer and tighter than if built by ordinary cut-to-fit methods. Waste in material cannot occur. Every inch of lumber you pay for is actually in and a part of your house. You know the lumber that's wasted costs just as much as the lumber that's used. The average house built by the old way wastes 18 per cent of the lumber—$18 out of every $100 of your money is wasted—burned up for kindling wood.

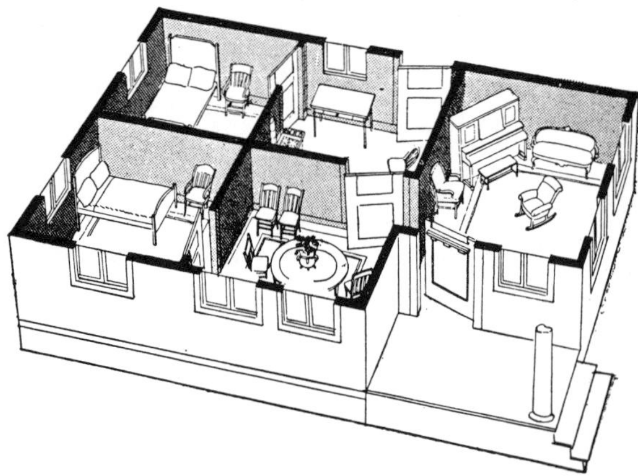

The Castle is shown here setting the narrow way on the lot. It can, of course, be placed the wide way to the street without changing the plans. In this case the steps would be placed on the other side of the porch.

Let us tell you more about this home. Write us today and we will send you complete detail descriptions and specifications.

See Terms on page 2 and General Specifications on pages 12 and 13.

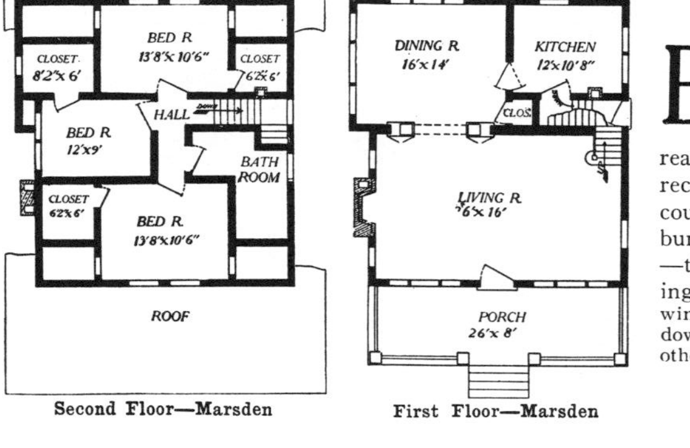

Second Floor—Marsden

First Floor—Marsden

The Marsden $1,396.50

Price, $1,470.00
Cash discount, 5%
Net price, $1,396.50

EACH year the sales of this attractive semi-bungalow far exceed the preceding year, and best of all its rapidly increasing number of owners are invariably delighted with their new home. We wish you could read some of the entertaining letters, without solicitation, received from scores of Marsden owners. They will of course be sent on request. Just study the lines of this bungalow and note how artistically appointed is every part, —the straight line dormer with exposed eaves in exact keeping with the eave of the front porch—the extended bay window with roof and brackets, breaking the gable end—the windows of different sizes and styles and location—these and many other points make the exterior of the Marsden truly artistic.

In interior planning and arrangement, this modern bungalow presents what might well be said to be the last word in designing. On entering the large living room, 26x16, extending across the entire front, one is attracted by the beautiful bookcase arch separating the living and dining rooms. Beautiful in itself, yet this arch by means of its glass doors and adjustable shelves forms at once a convenient, attractive and useful piece of house furnishing. Notice the abundance of light in living and dining rooms. A well arranged kitchen with stairs leading to grade landing complete the first floor. Ascending to the second floor by the semi-open stairs at the end of living room, one enters a central hall from which easy access is gained to each of the three large bedrooms and the bath. Please note the clothes closet with each bedroom—a most appreciated adjunct for every sleeping room. The price includes everything above the foundation to complete the bungalow. Front steps, grade entrance and cellar stairs. Siding can be substituted if desired for wall shingles at no additional cost. See Terms on page 2 and General Specifications on pages 12 and 13.

The Venus
$848.35

Price, Size No. 1, $893.00
Cash discount, 5%
Net price, $848.35

Price, Size No. 2, $1,018.00
Cash discount, 5%
Net price, $967.10

ONE of our customers wrote us saying: "It has been a never ending pleasure to me to see the effect of my Venus home on the passers-by. It continually attracts attention from people riding and walking by, many of whom stop to take a second look."

We were greatly pleased to receive this letter because our aim when designing this house was to **make it** unusually attractive.

The Venus is a type of home that appears equally as well on a narrow lot as one that has plenty of frontage.

A careful study of the exterior shows that many artistic touches have been added to get this effect. The most noticeable features are the casement windows, heavy brackets supporting the eaves, exposed rafter ends and the bracket hoods over the front bedroom windows.

The porch is unique and unusual in shape with a combination gable and drop roof effect.

From the porch the living-room is entered directly, and you will be surprised at the spaciousness. The windows on the three sides light it admirably. The living and dining rooms are separated by an attractive cased arch, while a swinging door connects the dining room and kitchen. See photos of interior of Venus on page 71.

A grade cellar door at the side gives access to kitchen and cellar. On the second floor the bedrooms and bath open directly into the hall. The rooms have slightly sloping ceilings near the side walls, but the slope is so slight that it does not detract from the appearance of the rooms nor interfere with the placing of furniture.

We have on file some interesting information and suggestions for interior decorations for every room in the home. Also have figures on the cost of erection from top of foundation to the time of completion or occupancy.

We will gladly send it to you at your request.

First Floor Plan The Venus No. 2

Second Floor Plan The Venus No. 2

See General Specifications on pages 12 and 13. See Terms on page 2. See Interior Illustrations, page 71.

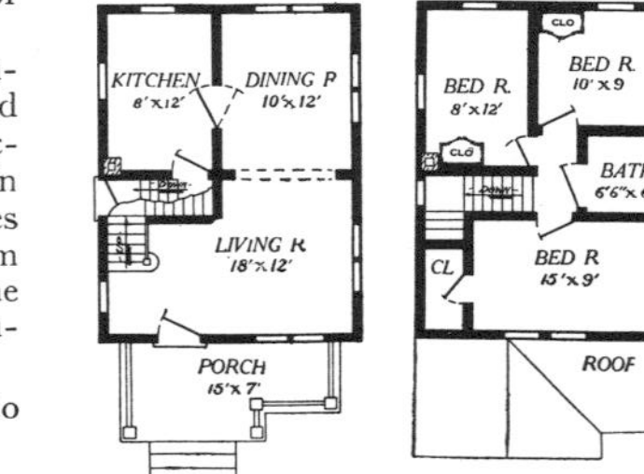

First Floor Plan The Venus No. 1

Second Floor Plan The Venus No. 1

The Princeton — A Complete Cottage

A COSY, comfortable, convenient, warm home; that exactly describes this remarkable house. It is as good a building in every sense of the word for its size as money can buy, and when erected is worth $1,200 to $1,400. It is designed and built exactly like any good contractor would build it. Identically the same beautiful interior finish and knotless lumber goes into the construction of the Princeton as into our most expensive houses. It simply cannot be surpassed. This house can be put up and completed by two inexperienced men ready to be papered and painted in about ten days. This is possible because every stick is cut the right size and ready to be nailed in place, and because our instructions and drawings are so complete that no sawing, figuring or fussing is necessary. Every piece in the house is marked to correspond with the drawings. Study the floor plan and see how conveniently the house is laid out. Note the arch between living room and dining room, large porch, the cellar entrance, etc. A careful study of the arrangement of rooms will show convenience at every point. Price of Princeton No. 2, $720.00. Cash discount, 5%. Net price, $684.00.

See Terms on page 2 and General Specifications on pages 12 and 13.

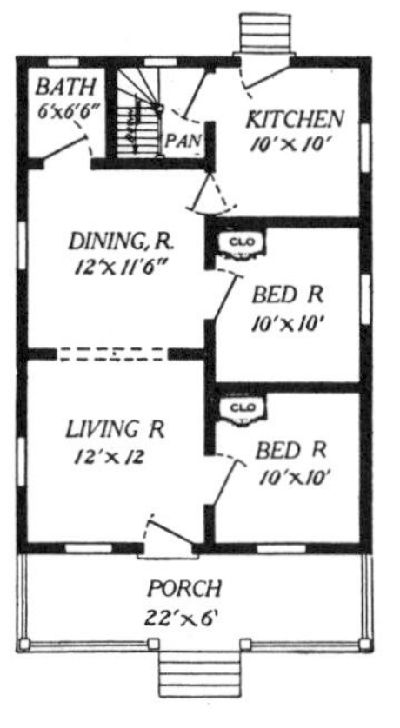

Floor Plan
The Princeton No. 1

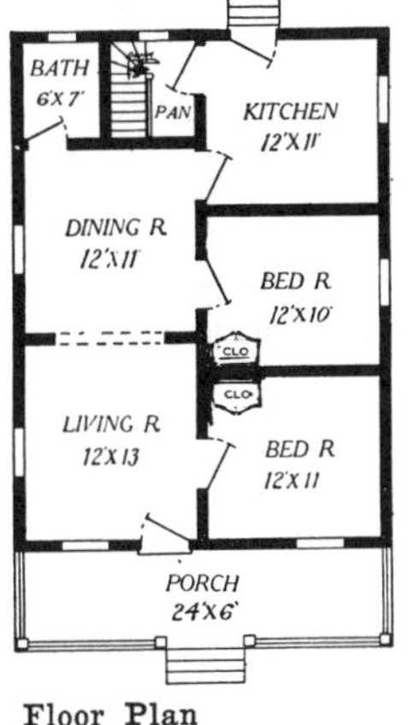

Floor Plan
The Princeton No. 2

$598.50

Price, No. 1, $630.00
Cash discount, 5%
Net price, $598.50

The Virginia  $1,197.00

Price, $1,260.00
Cash discount, 5%
Net price, $1,197.00

HERE'S a home. From every view it breathes a welcome, inviting you into its big, strong, protecting walls to find comfort, pleasure, and satisfaction. From the front it strikes you pleasingly, and, as you approach, the impression is heightened by the finished detail of roof, eaves, columns, and porch work.

The exterior of the Virginia always pleases—the design being founded on conservative lines. The wide porch stretching across the front is always a popular feature, especially the one designed for the Virginia. Slender spindles are extended from the rail to the ground creating a very neat appearance. The bay at the side breaks the long straight sidewall, thus adding attractiveness to the exterior and providing a cosy corner for the interior. The special

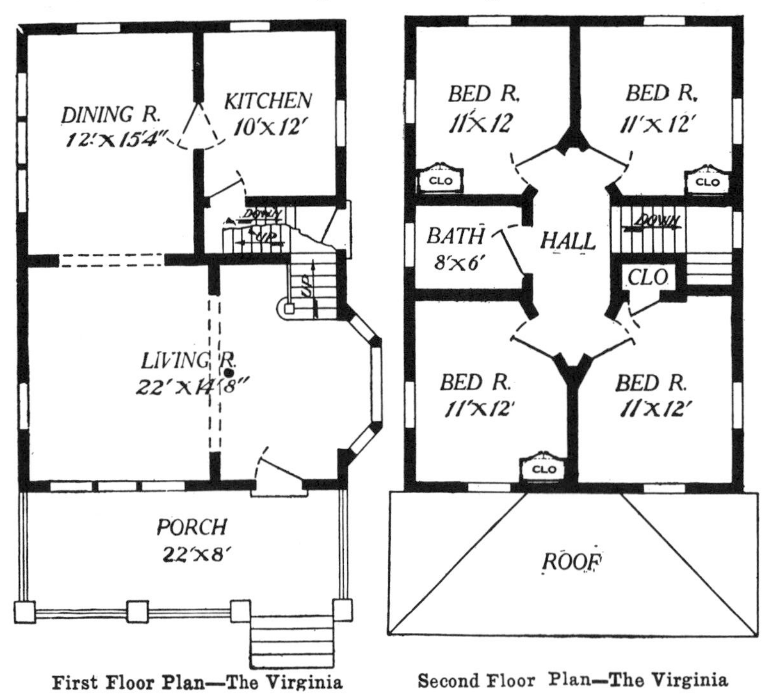

First Floor Plan—The Virginia

Second Floor Plan—The Virginia

scrolled bracket which is used for decoration under eaves of house roof and dormer roof add a touch of beauty to the home.

The Virginia as shown here is painted gray with white trim. Many other attractive schemes could be used with equal or greater success. The belt dividing first and second stories suggest a dark color—possibly brown for second story and cream for first story, with white trim.

The Virginia is a popular design among Aladdin customers. It has been erected many times thruout the country. Owners are loud in their praise of it. Dr. Corn of Ohio, writes as follows: "The material was excellent and every piece fitted exactly."

Mr. J. F. Kugler of Pennsylvania, in a letter says: "I saved between $300 and $500. I have a fine home—The Virginia."

Mrs. M. E. Lloyd, of Florida, who has erected two Aladdins, in a letter says: "Everything went together like clock-work. My Virginia is a fine home."

Just inspect the arrangement of the interior. A living room that stretches from the bay window on one side of the house to the other, twenty-two feet, with the dining room separated by a wide arch—a freedom and expanse usually found only in much larger houses. One of the most interesting features on the interior is the bay window. This is most usually converted into a cozy corner and fitted with window seat, sofa cushions, etc., making it the most popular part of the home. The cozy corner in bay window and handsome open stairway make a pleasing impression on entering the home. Kitchen, four bedrooms, bath, and closets complete this beautiful home. It is built to satisfy the hardest to please. It is a continual delight to every owner.

See Terms on page 2 and General Specifications on pages 12 and 13.

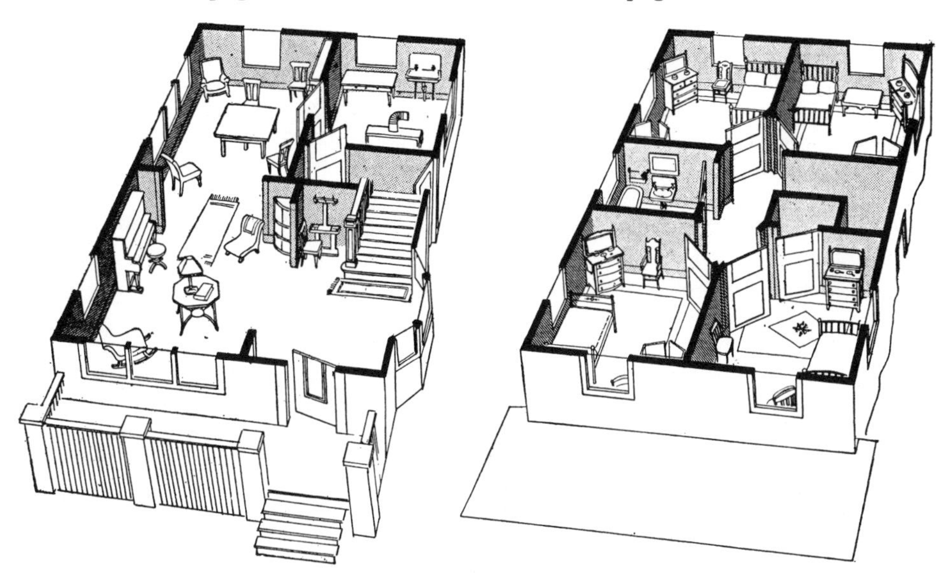

The New Eden $645.05

Price, $679.00
Cash discount, 5%
Net price, $645.05

THIS home, the New Eden, shows the result of careful planning before building—and it is surely gratifying to its many owners among Aladdin customers. On a ground space of 20x20 feet, this home gives more room, more comfort, more convenience than has ever before been obtained. Two stories, having two bedrooms upstairs, a hall, a living room, a dining room, a kitchen, an open stairway, a porch, and above all, an attractive looking house. It is so well liked by its many happy owners, that it is common for them to call it the "Wonder Home" on account of its low price, abundance of space, and its convenience.

Notice the exterior. A broad belt across the front of the house divides first and second stories, giving a pleasing and harmonious effect. The half-sheltered porch is a pleasant feature and is well built for strength, attractiveness and harmony. The full length column, fronted by pedestals, makes a comfortable porch. The diamond paned window to the left of the front door gives plenty of light to the stairway and adds attractiveness to the front of the house and porch. Living room and dining room are divided by a wide arch, making them practically one room. Both rooms are well lighted and of good size. Notice the double window in the dining room. Two men can erect and complete this house in about ten days. It can be done by any two men who are willing to work, assisted by our complete instructions and illustrations. See General Specifications on pages 12 and 13. Detail specifications will be sent you on request. See Terms on page 2.

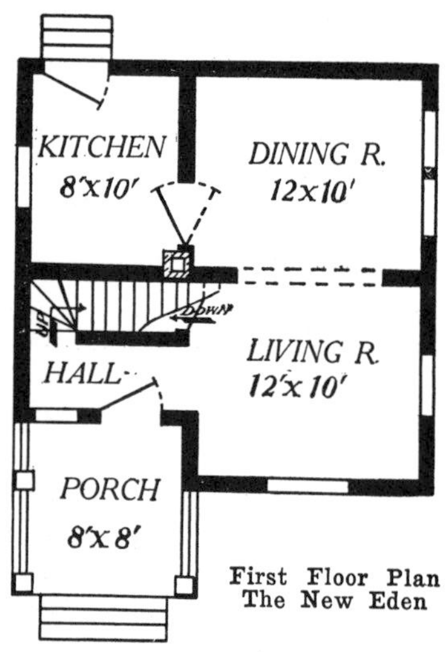

First Floor Plan
The New Eden

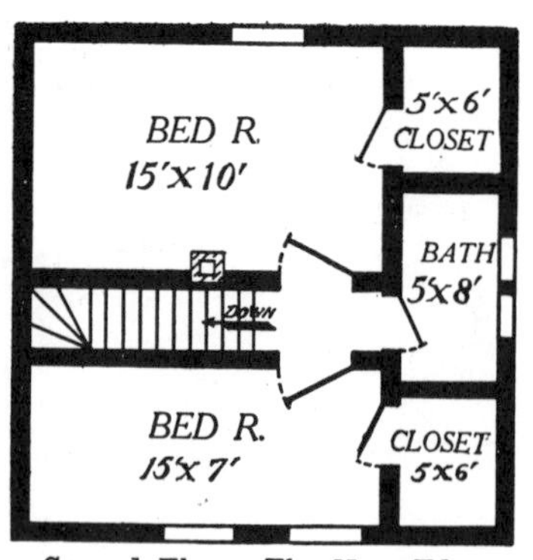

Second Floor—The New Eden

Living Room-The Wilmont
Dining Room-The Wilmont
Living Room-The Roseland
Living Room and Dining Room
- The Detroit -

The Hudson $1,098.20

Price, $1,156.00
Cash discount, 5%
Net price, $1,098.20

CAN you imagine a better utilization of space than is obtained in the plan of the Hudson? The constant thought of Aladdin designers is toward giving a maximum of convenience and comfort for the lowest possible cost. It is doubtful if this result has been exceeded by any other Aladdin house. The exterior will please you, we are sure, as this home has a greater number of admirers. The Design is practical and conservative with no sign of over-trimming being evident. Simple lines in the porch construction, heavy overhead boxing, and roof are in perfect harmony with the balance of the home. The windows of both first

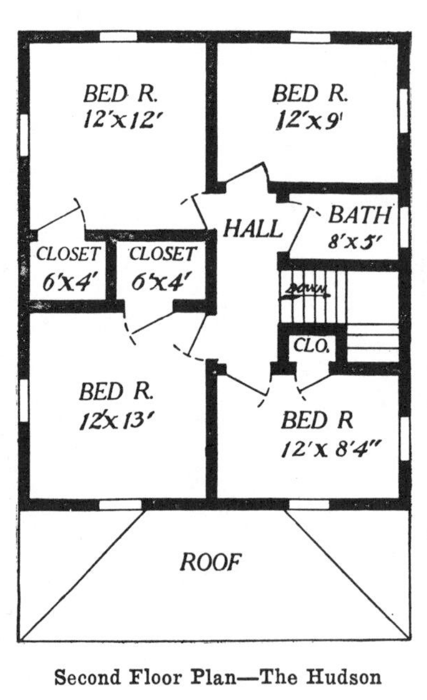

Second Floor Plan—The Hudson

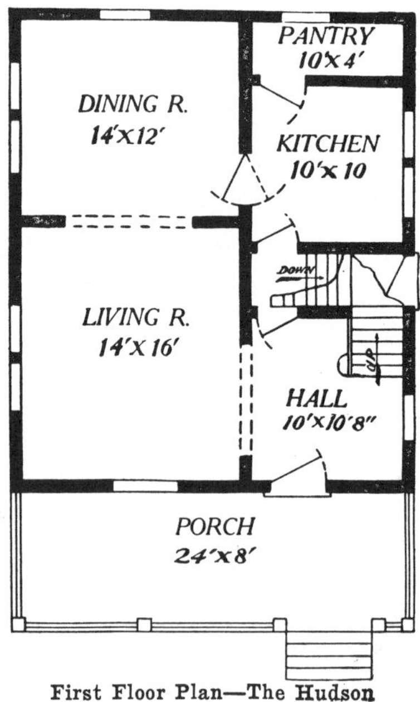

First Floor Plan—The Hudson

and second story are treated somewhat differently from the average. On the first floor the windows are capped by the wide belt dividing first and second floor. The windows on the second floor line up to the trim board under eaves.

The wide belt dividing first and second stories adds much to the general appearance of the Hudson.

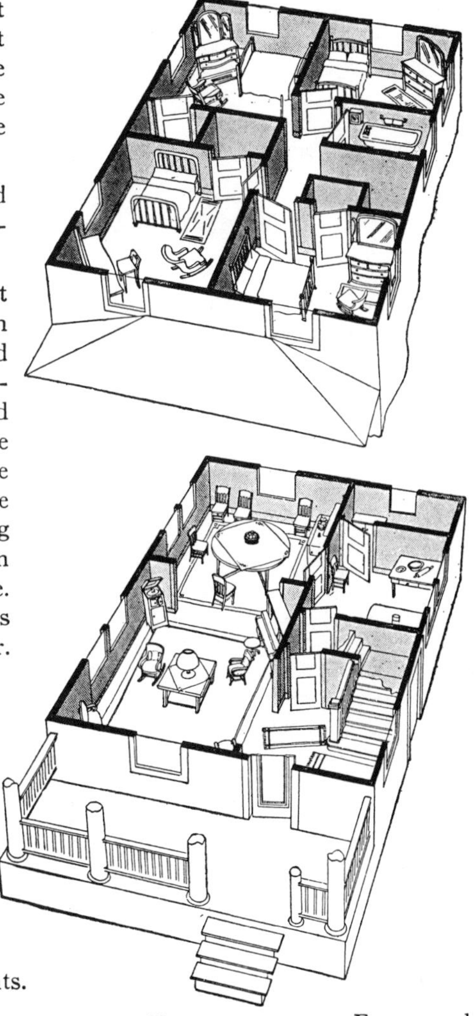

Notice the hip roof dormer on the front roof. It helps break up the flat plain roof. Study the location of rooms and the placing of doors and windows. Hudsons have been erected in many cities and towns about the country and you may be sure that each creates much favorable comment by friends and neighbors of the owners. The arches dividing hall, living room and dining room give an impression of size and space that is most desirable. The reception hall permits direct access to kitchen, living room, or second floor. Ample light for hallway and staircase is provided by full size window and three-quarter length glass in front door.

By referring to the plan you will find there is a stretch of space twenty-eight feet thru living room and dining room. The large living room, size 14x16 feet will prove interesting to you with the many possibilities for attractive furniture arrangements.

Entrance from hall to kitchen saves the housewife many steps. Four good bedrooms, closets and bath are arranged on the second floor. Four Colonial columns support the porch roof and a beautiful glass front door throws light into the hall, in addition to the side window, and the woodwork and floors are of the beautiful grained Western fir which is subject to any treatment you like. To lovers of simplicity in home architecture the Hudson always appeals strongly.

We have many interesting letters from Hudson owners telling of their experiences, cost of erection, and length of time in building. We will be glad to send you copies of these letters or will send you names and addresses of owners nearest you. In this way you can write and learn at first hand of their complete satisfaction.

See Specifications on pages 12 and 13.

20° Below Zero—Hudson Warm and Comfortable

My "Hudson" purchased last year was very warm and comfortable this winter when the thermometer was twenty degrees below zero. The lumber was first-class and I am more than satisfied with my home. Everything was found as represented and no knots to be seen. If I were to build again I would build another Aladdin.—H. M. Pierce.

The Brentwood $2,185.00

Price, $2,300.00
Cash discount, 5%
Net price, $2,185.00

Reception Hall—The Brentwood

THIS most charming dwelling has a host of admirers. Its individuality is apparent in many ways. The broken roof, second story balcony, hooded front entrance, semi-enclosed porch, pergola porte-cochere with French doors leading to dining-room, casement windows in front and full attic, form a delightfully attractive whole. The house will be furnished with either siding, shingles, or stucco exterior. The bay window projects three feet and is ten feet wide. The pergola at the side is furnished with tin roof, giving protection against snow and rain. This pergola can be furnished with floor, giving a side veranda instead of porte-cochere. A most unusual and distinctive idea is the little balcony with double French doors from the upper sewing room.

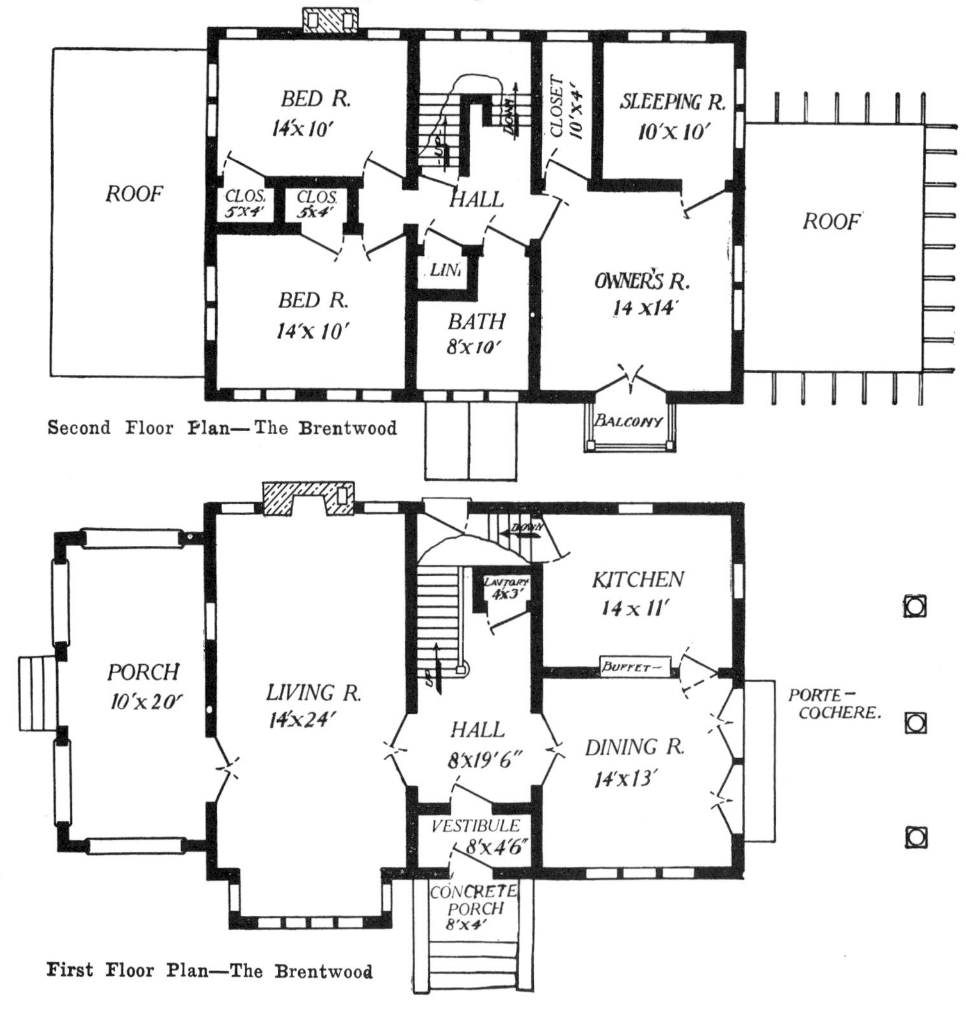

Second Floor Plan—The Brentwood

First Floor Plan—The Brentwood

Note the sleeping room leading from sitting or dressing room on second floor. This gives all the advantages of the sleeping porch, with none of its inconveniences. This sleeping room has four windows. Linen closet is arranged in hall, a very large closet from the sewing room, and each bedroom has a closet. The hall, both first and second story, is commodious, while a stairway of pure Colonial type is furnished. Built-in buffet in dining room affords room for dishes, linen, and silver.

A Tennessee owner (name upon request) writes about his Brentwood: "My Brentwood is the admiration of the town. It was ready for plastering two weeks after the first nail was driven. I saved about $700 with Aladdin's help." Could you wish for greater assurance of your own satisfaction than from the pen of this owner?

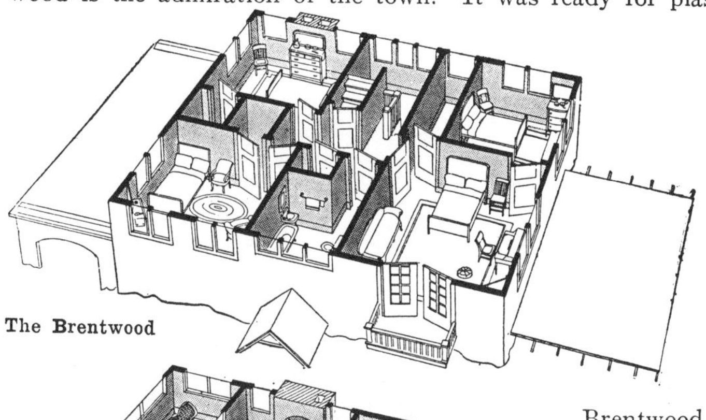

The Brentwood

The Brentwood is erected in many states over the country. It is also erected in Bay City, Michigan, the Home office of Aladdin houses. We invite you to pay a visit to one of the Brentwood homes nearest you, or if you should visit near Bay City we would be pleased to arrange a visit for you. This remarkable home will surely interest you and we are positive you would be delighted with an inspection of it. Should you desire to write an owner of the Brentwood asking him his experiences we will be glad to furnish names.

See Terms on page 2 and General Specifications on pages 12 and 13.

The Sunshine $1,096.30

Price, $1,154.00
Cash discount, 5%
Net price, $1,096.30

THIS charming bungalow nestling in this setting of trees represents one of the best pieces of work of our master designers.

Individuality is portrayed in all its lines and it is distinctively American in character.

Extreme simplicity is the motif behind the planning of this home.

Simplicity implies character, quality and taste.

Sunshine implies cheerfulness, happiness, prosperity and light.

Could a more fitting name than "Sunshine" be given to this home?

It radiates that sweet, simple home atmosphere everyone wishes to secure in their home and to see in the homes of others.

The roof lines are particularly graceful, the main roof extending down over the porch, it being evenly balanced by a dormer of just the right proportions.

A study of the interior reveals an exceptionally well laid and thought out plan.

Light in any home is an essential feature and we have provided an abundance of it for every room. The large living room gives access to the dining room and front bedroom, as well as small clothes closet. The opening between the living room and dining room is a prepossessing cased archway. The fireplace and outside chimney are shown in the photograph and floor plan although it is not necessary that you build these should you favor this house. One of the closettes as shown on page 115 is furnished for the front bedroom. The two back bedrooms have regular closets built off of them.

At the rear of the bungalow one of our regular Addition No. 4 is furnished, this providing for a combined cellar and rear entrance.

If the "Sunshine" appeals to you, write us so we can send you still further details. See Terms on page 2. Specifications on pages 12 and 13.

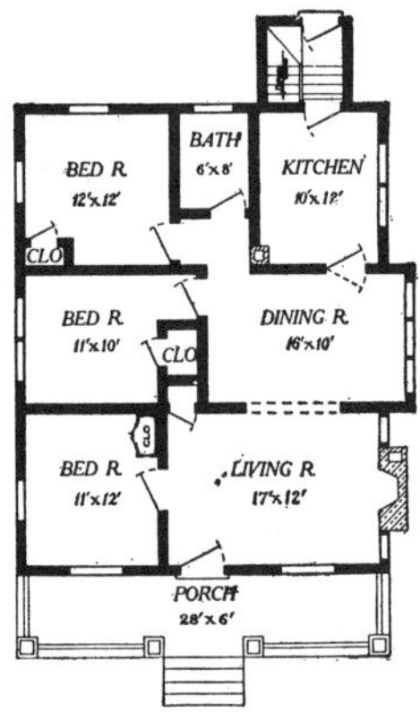

The Sunshine Floor Plan

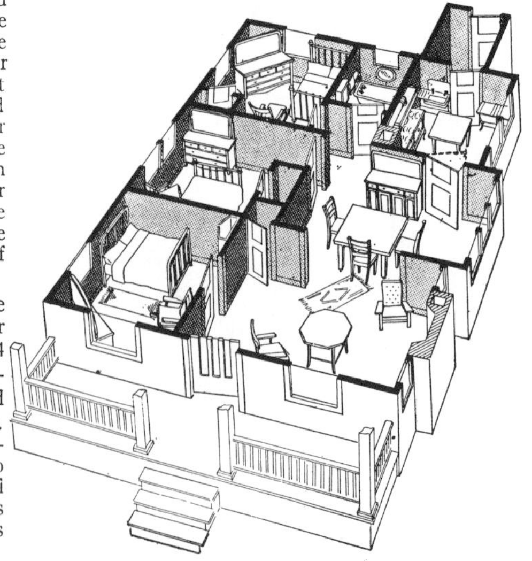

The Boulevard $898.70

Price, $946.00
Cash discount, 5%
Net price, $898.70

THE Boulevard is the wonder home to many prospective home-builders. The design in both exterior appearance and interior convenience is the result of deep thought in planning. Stop and think of it—three large bedrooms, large living room and dining room with good sized kitchen, bath and closets—and all on one floor! Of course, this number of rooms may be included in other one-story designs, but look again at the sizes of the rooms!

In point of design, The Boulevard is one of the most attractive. Designed on conservative lines, this home is marked by a number of pleasant architectural features. The dormer in the front roof gives light and air to attic and adds much to its beauty.

The porch is formed under the main roof—its wide dimensions provide comfort and add much to the general effect of this home.

A wide belt divides the siding on the first story and shingles in gable—the treatment used here is excellent, white belt, brown stained shingles and sidewalls.

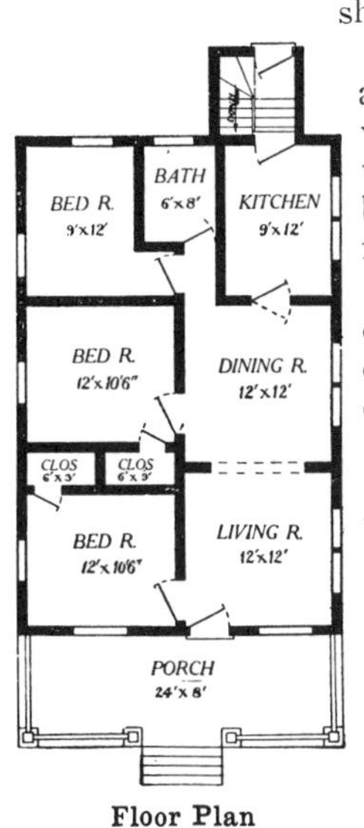

Floor Plan
The Boulevard

The interior will appeal to every housewife who has a desire to make the home beautiful and comfortable.

The arrangement of rooms and size of each permit excellent decoration and the utmost in convenience. See Interior Illustrations page 71.

Study General Specifications on pages 12 and 13. Complete detail specifications will be sent you upon request.

See Terms on page 2.

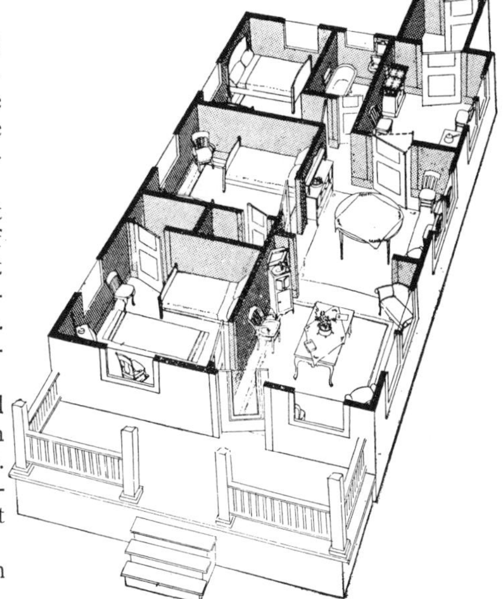

Shadow Lawn $1,539.00

Price, $1,620.00
Cash discount, 5%
Net price, $1,539.00

DID you ever see a more beautiful picture of its kind than the one shown here? A mass of lights and shadows softening the greens, browns and grays of the foliage shingles and cobbles delights the eye. You can almost feel the touch of the sunbeams patterning the lawn, and you just want to stroll up the steps and into the inviting shade of the porch. Most effectively has the pure white that borders

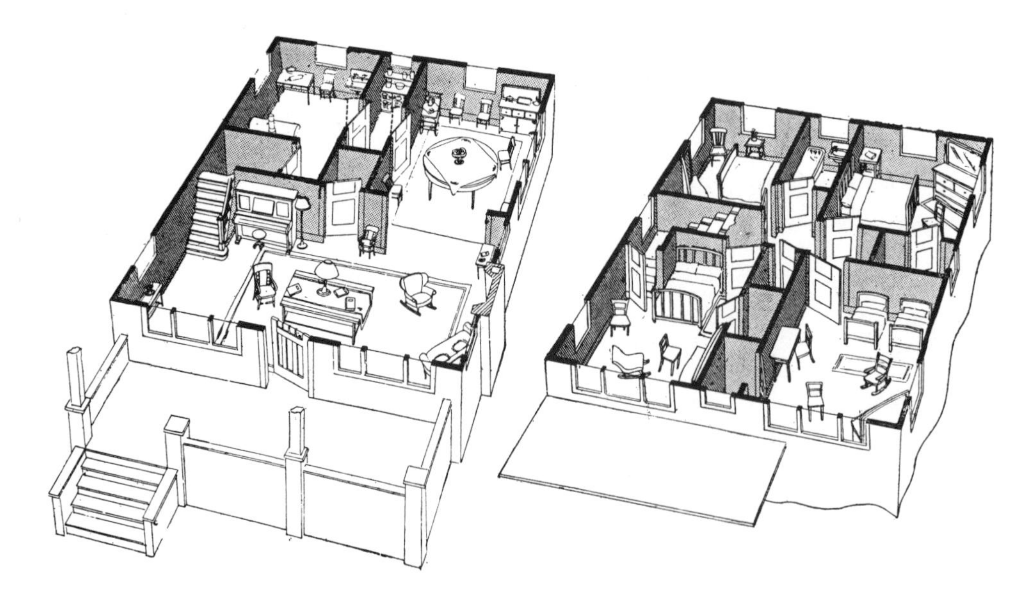

every outline been used to contrast the deep brown of the shingled upper story.

Examining further we find a living room of expansive dimensions, twenty-eight feet one way and fourteen feet the other. Matching the size of the living room is a dining room sixteen feet in depth and twelve feet broad; large enough for a real banquet. The kitchen, pantry and grade entrance occupy the other rear half.

The second story illustrates four bedrooms, bath and closets.

The Shadow Lawn eaves project four feet, rather a Swiss idea, and are supported by well proportioned brackets. The porte cochere at the left is not included in the price quoted. Should you desire it added to the home it is furnished readi-cut at the extra price of $94.00. The Shadow Lawn is surely a home of most striking individuality.

See Terms on page 2 and General Specifications on pages 12 and 13.

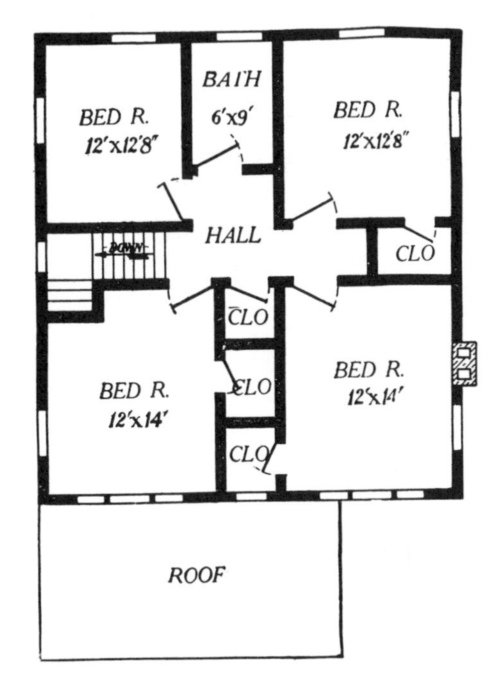

Second Floor Plan—Shadow Lawn

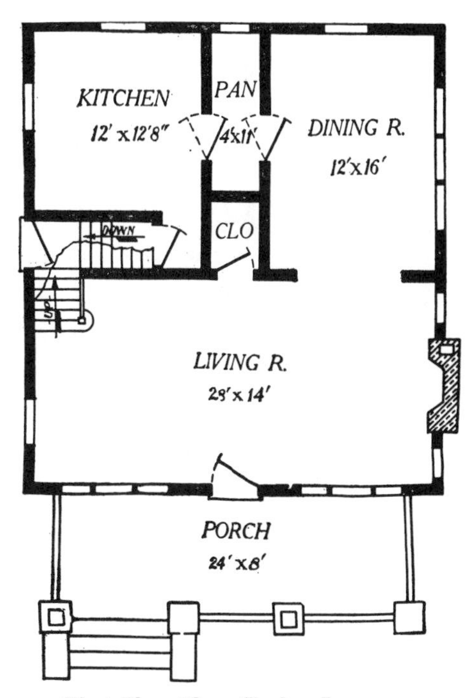

First Floor Plan—Shadow Lawn

The Sheridan Two Sizes $1,059.25

Price, No. 1, $1,115.00
Cash discount, 5%
Net price, $1,059.25

AN unusually attractive exterior and a sense of roominess are features that make the Sheridan one of our most popular bungalows. The low, sloping roof, the scrolled eaves and shingled porch and step rails, together with the siding, permit a great latitude in the decorative scheme and with the use of harmonious painting and staining materials, these features can be developed in a most pleasing manner. The expansive porch, which extends across the entire front, is well shaded by the broad overhanging roof.

Two convenient and inviting arrangements of the several rooms are outlined below. Your attention is called to the square and good dimensions of all the rooms, especially the living room, with its attractive group windows and arch leading to the dining room. Divided square lights are furnished for upper square sash of all windows, although they will be furnished with single large glass if preferred.

The exterior details for both the Sheridan No. 1 and No. 2 are practically the same with the probable exception of location of windows. The bay window is a feature included only with the Sheridan No. 2 and is built off the

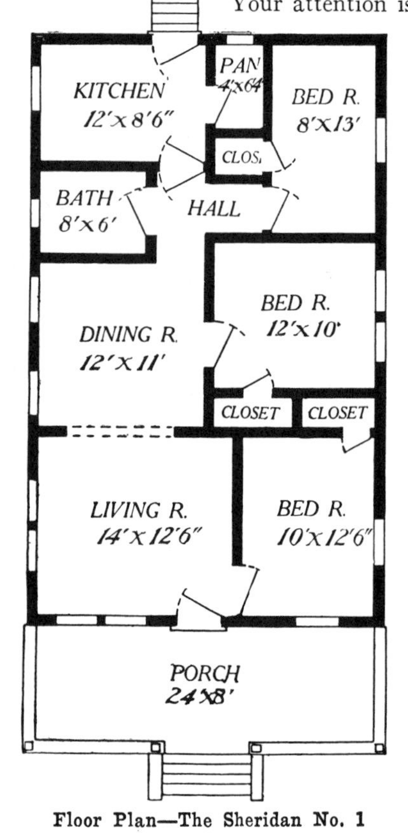

Floor Plan—The Sheridan No. 1

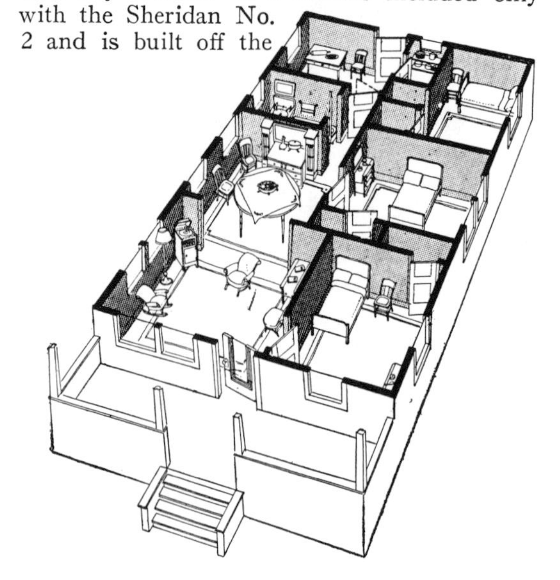

dining room. A fireplace is shown in the living room of floor plan No. 2. This may be omitted if desired. The floor plan of the Sheridan No. 1 doesn't show fireplace; however, it may be included if desired.

The Sheridan No. 1 plan is very compact and convenient. It is not quite as large as the No. 2 plan; however, the arrangement of rooms, sizes, etc., have proven very popular among our customers. A large living and dining room are divided by the handsome wide cased arch. A short hallway between dining room and kitchen also leads to the bathroom and rear bedroom.

Porch, The Sheridan

The kitchen is of ample size and has proven very popular among housewives. Pantry with window is situated off the kitchen. Three good sized bedrooms with closets complete the plan of Sheridan No. 1.

The Sheridan No. 2 is two feet wider and four feet longer than plan No. 1. Of course, the rooms are larger in some instances, which proves more desirable to a number of our builders. Some of the features to be had in plan No. 2 are the bay window in dining room and grade cellar entrance of kitchen. The windows shown on each side of the fireplace in plan No. 2 are of the casement type and are much smaller than the regular size. This provides space for built-in bookcases on either side of the fireplace. If you do not wish the fireplace in the living room the regular style two-sliding sash will be furnished.

On an average, owners of the Sheridan claim savings of $300 to $425 on their homes. These estimates include savings on cost of material, also savings on cost of labor. When you receive the material it is entirely cut-to-fit, ready for erection. You pay for only the actual material used in building your home—no more. Now, think of the good lumber that is wasted in building the old-fashioned way. And you also pay for the extra labor which is unnecessary building an Aladdin.

Ask for names of customers living near you. Let them tell you in their own words.

Sheridan No. 2, price, $1260.00, cash discount 5%. Net price, $1,197.00

Few moderately priced bungalows offer so many real home comforts as can be found in the Sheridan.

See Terms on page 2 and General Specifications on pages 12 and 13.

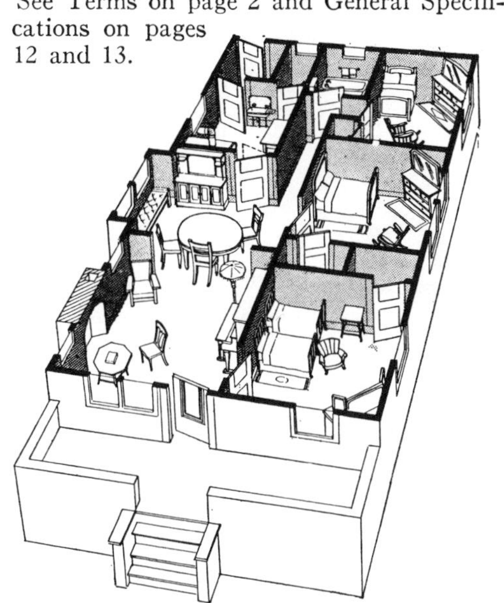

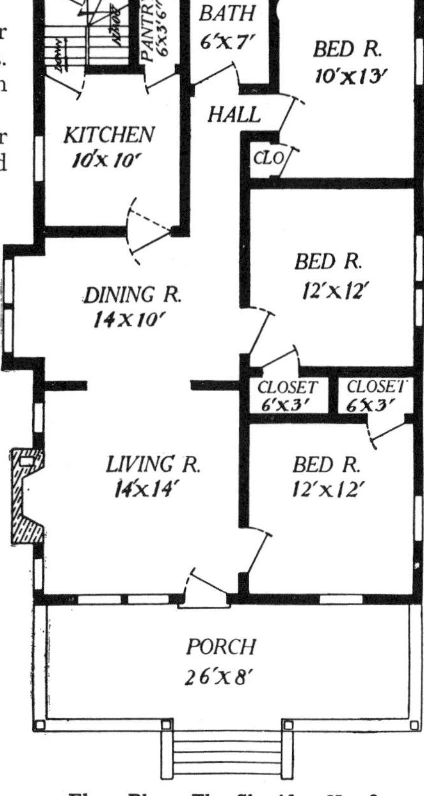

Floor Plan—The Sheridan No. 2

The Finley $765.70

Price, $806.00
Cash discount, 5%
Net price, $765.70

WHILE the Finley is popular with the owner of any sized lot, yet it finds special favor in cities where lots are sometimes as narrow as 30, or even 25 feet. The Finley can be built very nicely on a 25-foot lot and still leave ample space for a walk on either side.

In the Finley the architect has followed throughout plain, straight lines, yet when painted French gray or leather brown and trimmed in white, the owner of the Finley is invariably delighted.

A large, pleasant front porch, six rooms, bath and closettes are found in this remarkably low priced house. The ever popular plan is followed of a large living room across the entire front with wide archway leading to dining room. By a double-action door one enters the kitchen direct from the dining room. An attractive semi-open stairs leads from living room to second floor where there are to be found three sleeping rooms, bath and closettes. Those wanting a six-room, two-story plain house are invariably pleased with the Finley. See Terms, page 2 and General Specifications, pages 12 and 13.

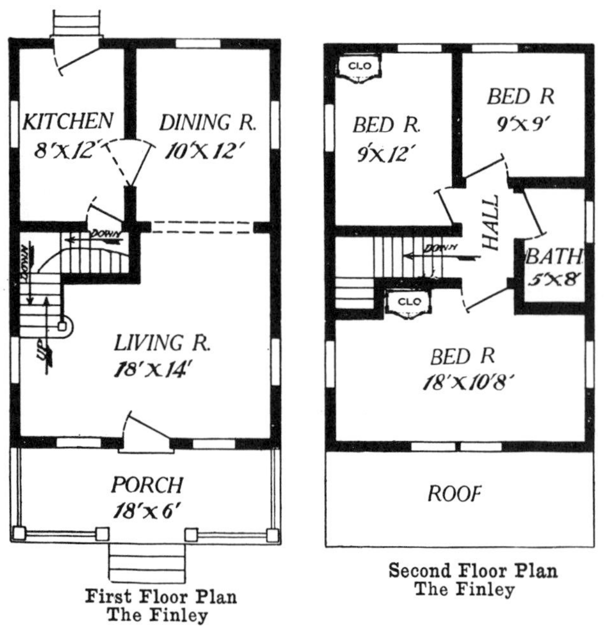

First Floor Plan
The Finley

Second Floor Plan
The Finley

The Tucson $495.90

Price, $522.00
Cash discount, 5%
Net price, $495.90

WHEN it comes to much in a small space the Tucson certainly leads. Five convenient, well lighted, attractive rooms, with good sized front porch make up this snug and cosy little home. Sash front door, semi-open stairs and wide arch between living room and dining room add materially to the attractiveness of the Tucson. Where the exterior is painted either a French gray or seal brown and trimmed with white or cream, and the beautifully grained interior fir trim is either finished with oil or stain and then varnished, the Tucson presents a fresh, attractive appearance that invariably brings pleasure and satisfaction to its owner. (Rear addition shown in photograph not included. See page 108.)

The Tucson is one of the first Aladdin designs and has always proven exceptionally popular. The first year it was listed in the Aladdin catalog it was sold to four different parties who have built the Tucson again after the first one was complete.

A number of companies have erected this house in large numbers. One customer in 1913 erected sixty-four.

At the price quoted you save between $150 to $275 on the material and erection of the Tucson. The material is prepared from carefully drawn plans—and without waste. Hence you pay for no lumber that is wasted in sawing or fitting on the ground. Your carpenters will be able to erect it much faster. This saving is also noticeable, as it usually cuts down time of erection a third.

Send for complete detailed specifications of the Tucson which will be sent to you upon request.

See Terms on page 2 and General Specifications on pages 12 and 13.

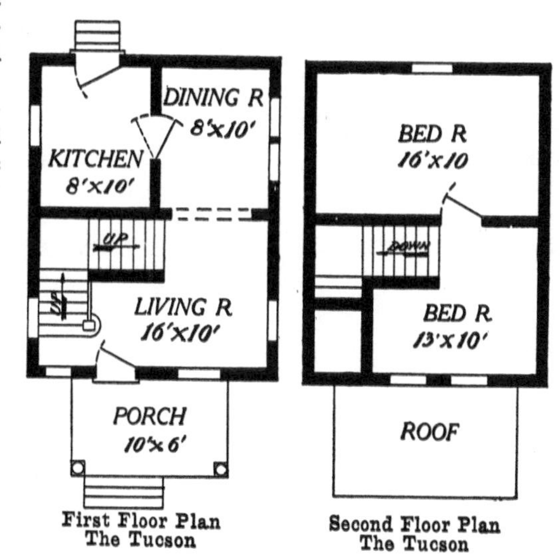

First Floor Plan
The Tucson

Second Floor Plan
The Tucson

The Hamilton $1,092.75

Price, $1,150.00
Cash discount, 5%
Net price, $1,092.75

THIS is a very popular type of house in the smaller cities. It is of the half-shingled style, with a gable roof, porch, and split-roof dormer. A wide belt separates the shingled second story from the sided first story. Attic is ventilated by a small gable window. Square columns rest on solid sided porch rail. It is one of the simplest and easiest to build of any of our two-story designs. The living room is of generous dimensions, and open stairway at the rear. Living room, bedroom, dining room, and kitchen are down stairs, and four bedrooms with closets and bath are upstairs.

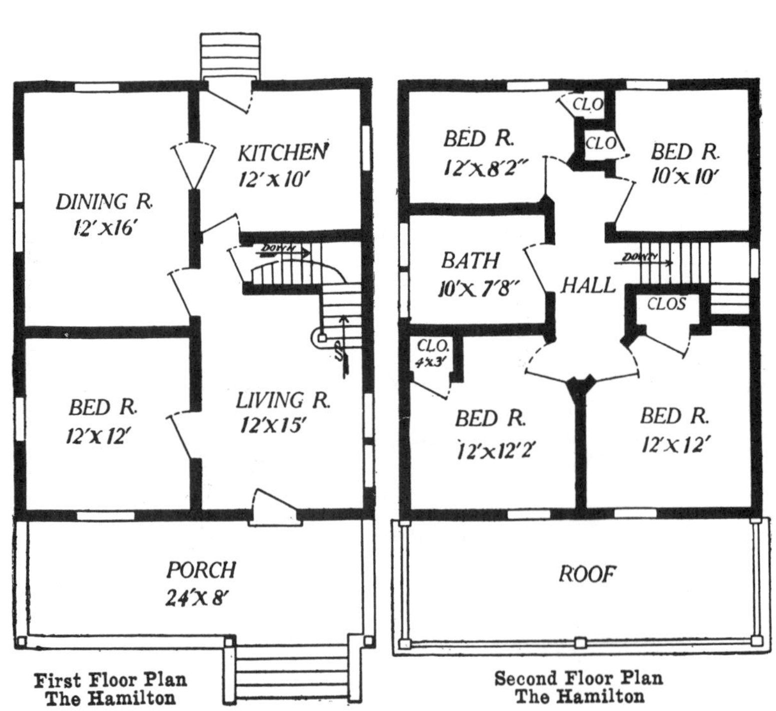

First Floor Plan
The Hamilton

Second Floor Plan
The Hamilton

See Terms on page 2 and General Specifications on pages 12 and 13.

Complete detailed specifications for the Hamilton will be sent to you upon request.

The Gretna $450.30

Price, $474.00
Cash discount, 5%
Net price, $450.30

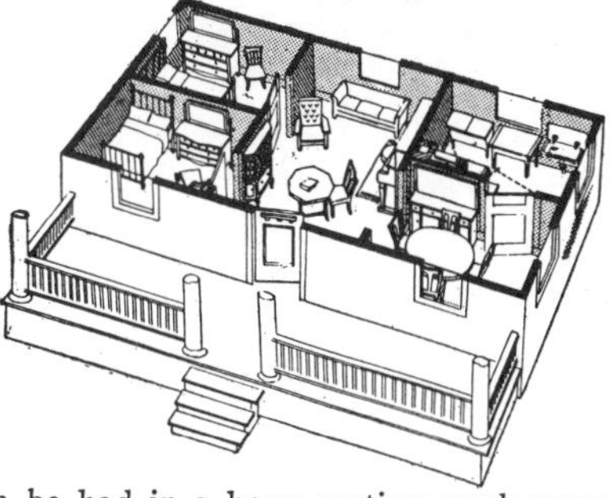

HERE is a complete five-room dwelling with all the beauty of simplicity of design. It has appealed so strongly to home builders and has met their needs so satisfactorily that you will find Gretnas scattered throughout the length and breadth of the land. It has been and is one of our very best sellers. The demand for it is constant. It is particularly desirable where ground space is not too expensive, as its width of thirty feet really requires a lot of forty feet or wider. Its long porch, sash door and casement windows give charm to the exterior, while the large living room, bedrooms, dining room and kitchen furnish as convenient and desirable an interior arrangement as can be had in a home costing much more money. Throughout you have the same excellent construction that is found in every Aladdin house, yet the lines of construction are so simple that scores of Gretna owners have built their entire house without any assistance from carpenters. The Gretna is distinctly a house for the home-loving man of moderate means, because without sacrificing attractiveness, convenience, or essentials, the cost has been brought within the reach of all. Either floor plan shown will be supplied at the same price. See General Specifications on pages 12 and 13 and Terms on page 2.

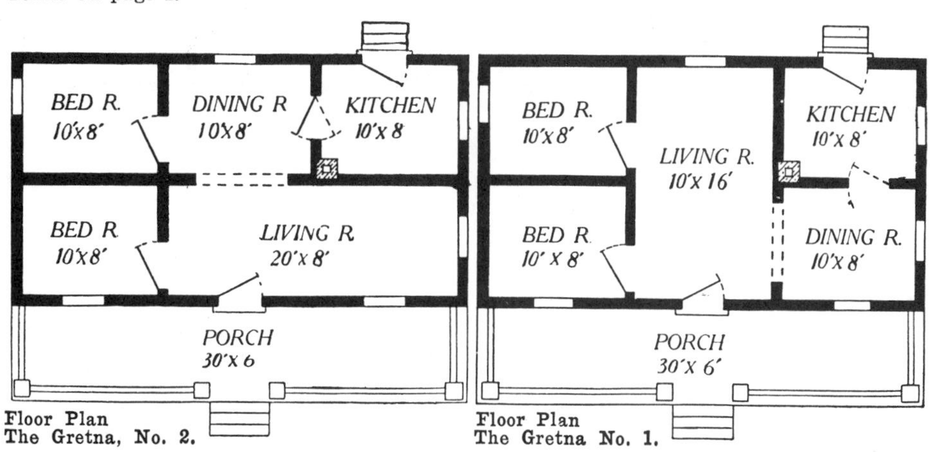

Floor Plan
The Gretna, No. 2.

Floor Plan
The Gretna No. 1.

The Pomona

One-Story **$1,296.75**

Price, $1,365.00
Cash discount, 5%
Net price, $1,296.75

Living Room—The Pomona

Dining Room—The Pomona (Paneling not included)

IF there is such a thing as personality in a home the Pomona surely expresses the feeling in every angle and line. Bathed in a hot summer sun's rays, its wide eaves, shady porch and many windows offer cooling protection; or blanketed by winter's snows it nestles snugly compact, and inviting the traveler to its protection. Walls of siding and shingles, building paper; sheathing, studding and lath and plaster are equally good non-conductors of heat and cold. Externally, many interesting ideas are worked out and each blends naturally into the whole. Observe the tapered porch pillars of stucco, surmounted by clean lined columns of the same design. The chimney outline matches this plan, as does the rafter ends and the pro-

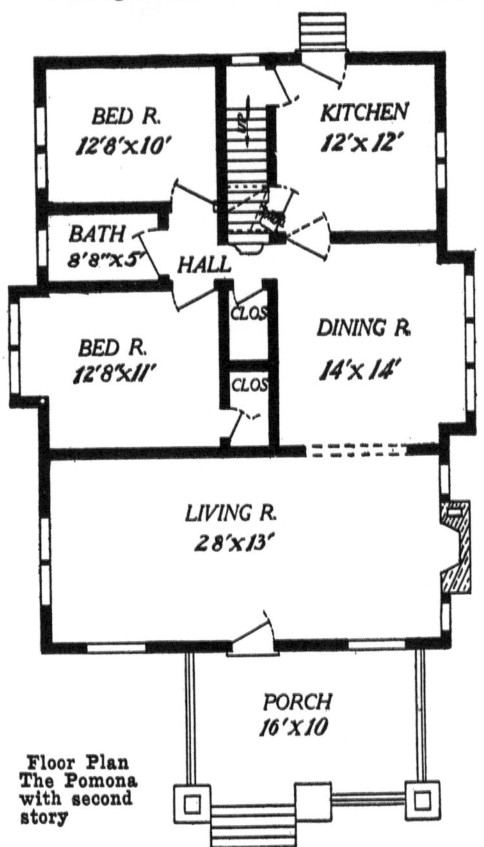

Floor Plan The Pomona with second story

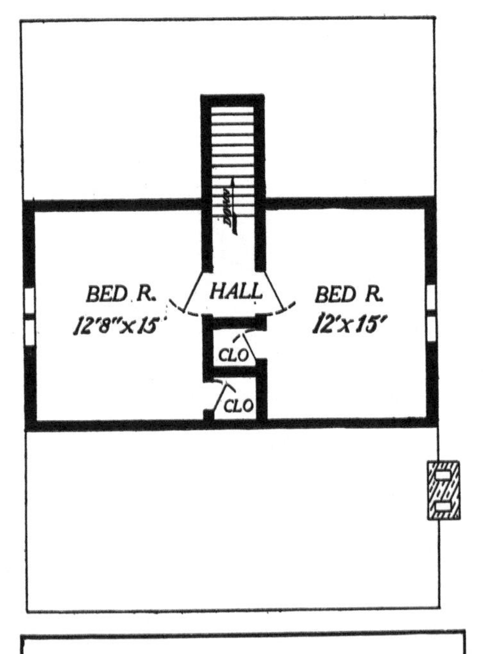

NOTE—There is no difference in outside dimensions of either Pomona plan. The only difference being a re-arrangement of the rooms and a second floor added, providing two extra bedrooms.

jecting ends of belt encircling the house above the water table. Brackets supporting the eaves are shaped differently than any other bungalow you ever saw, while the porch rail is embellished by a band running midway between the upper and lower rails. An especially notable feature of the interior arrangement is the abundance of unbroken wall spaces in all rooms. Can't you just imagine where you would place each piece of furniture? Two plans are illustrated, one-story and two-story. In the one-story, the front room is adaptable to use as den or bedroom, in the latter case giving three bedrooms. Good closets are observable in both designs. Price, two-story, $1,510. Net price, $1,434.50. See General Specifications on pages 12 and 13. Detail specifications for the Pomona will be sent on request. See Terms on page 2.

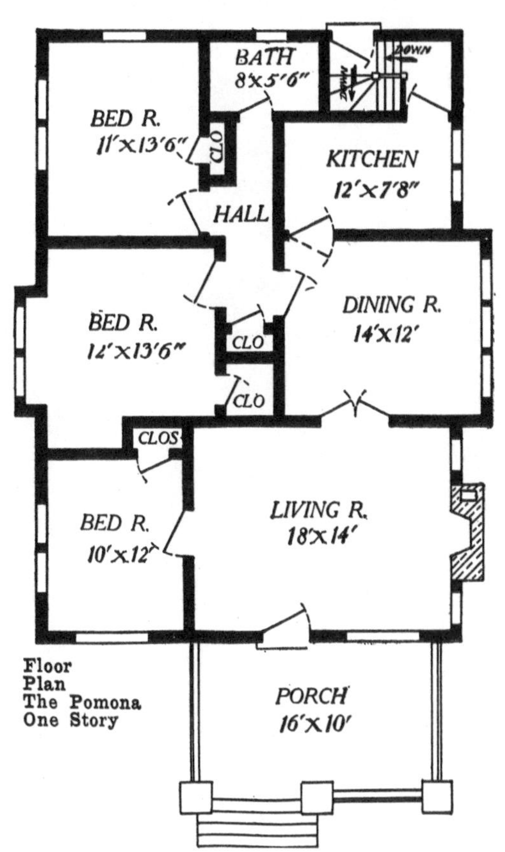

Floor Plan The Pomona One Story

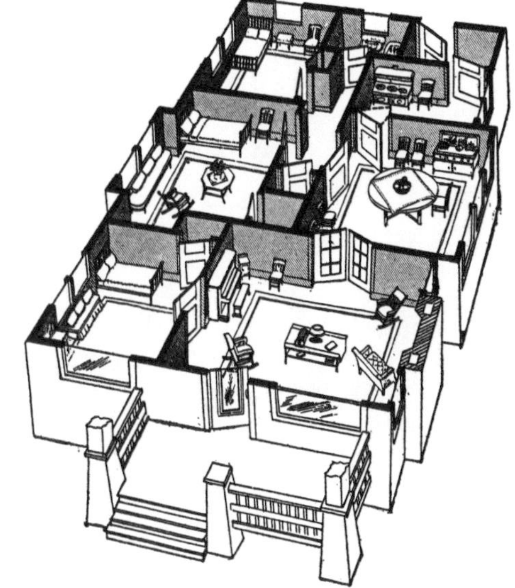

The Edison
$735.30

Price, $774.00
Cash discount, 5%
Net price, $735.30

BEFORE reading this description, what did you think of the Edison? Well, it has impressed others the same way—as being one of the prettiest little bungalows ever built. And every owner is more pleased with the Edison after it is completed. When the beautiful lines of this home are fully realized—then it is possible to see the broad and expansive porch sweeping across the entire front of the house, also the careful formation of the roof covering the porch. And did you notice the broad eaves with exposed rafters? This feature seems to belong to this home alone. And the diamond divided lights in the upper sash are in complete harmony with the balance of the beautiful home. Study the interior, the arrangement of rooms. Isn't it ideal? The living-room and dining-room, divided by an archway are really one big room, but still they retain the convenience of two. Each sleeping room affords plenty of air. The bathroom is well planned and is large enough for bathroom fixtures with plenty of space to spare.

For design, convenience and price, don't you think the Edison is the prettiest little bungalow you have seen? And when this bungalow is stained a dark brown and trimmed in pure white you have a most artistic and beautiful result.

See Terms on page 2 and General Specifications on pages 12 and 13.

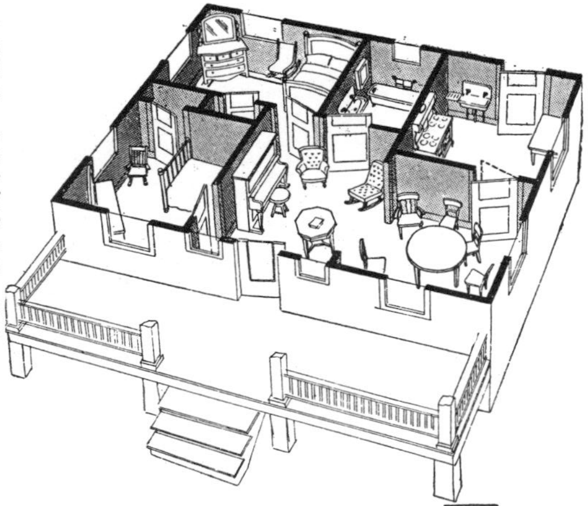

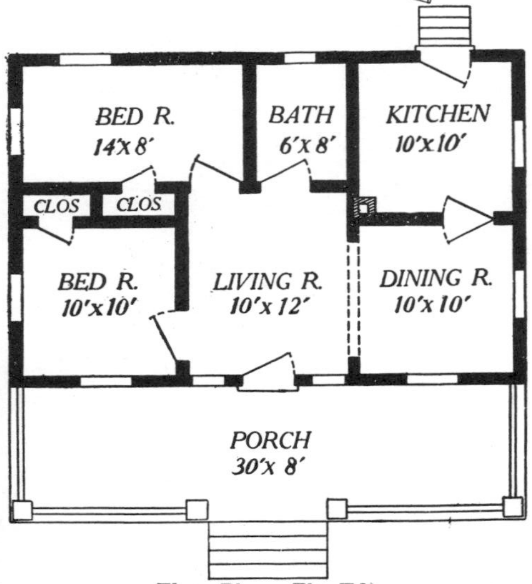

BED R. 14'x 8'
BATH 6'x 8'
KITCHEN 10'x 10'
CLOS
CLOS
BED R. 10'x 10'
LIVING R. 10'x 12'
DINING R. 10'x 10'
PORCH 30'x 8'

Floor Plan—The Edison

The Winthrop $996.55

Price, $1,049.00
Cash discount, 5%
Net price, $996.55

CAN you imagine this bungalow nestling among trees and shrubbery on your own lot? A few cobblestones are gathered from nearby fields and when blended with brown stained shingles, natural shrubbery and a setting of velvety green, the observer is fascinated.

A bungalow should always be set close to the ground. When local conditions seem to make this impossible, the same results can be secured by terracing close to the building.

The Winthrop is of the pure bungalow type—low, a touch of rough stones, bracketed eave supports, heavy timber work, shingles, and broken outlines.

And as the real bungalow is always compactly and conveniently arranged inside—you will agree that the Winthrop is typical. The large living room is lighted by three group windows and the fireplace at the end forms an inviting nook. Extra length is secured to the dining room by the interesting bay window. Lots of wall space is available in the front bedroom. The centralized hall, and entrance from dining room, kitchen, bath and bedroom is a good feature. Could a bathroom be better located than this? Rear porch with space for refrigerator, and grade cellar entrance. Can you help falling in love with this interesting bungalow?

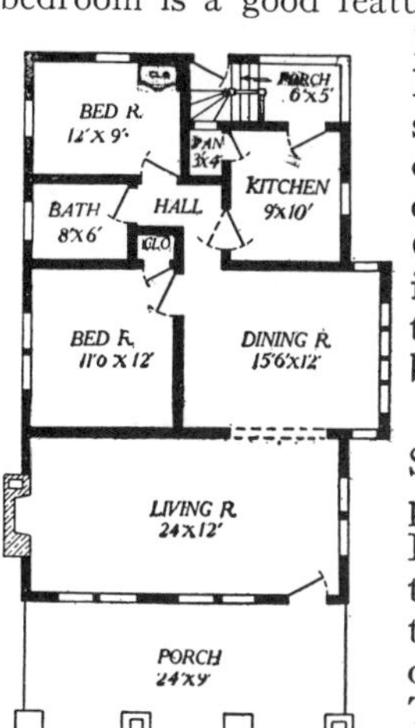

Floor Plan—The Winthrop

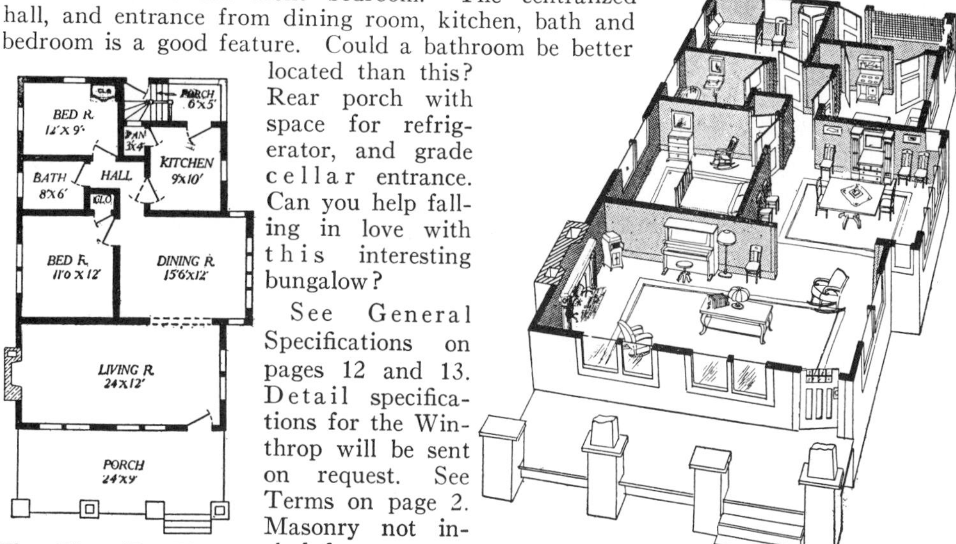

See General Specifications on pages 12 and 13. Detail specifications for the Winthrop will be sent on request. See Terms on page 2. Masonry not included.

The Charleston $1,472.50

Price, $1,550.00
Cash discount, 5%
Net price, $1,472.50

THERE are many good points in the Charleston, a modern square-type design. The first noticeable feature is the deep bay windows in front, both stories, also on one side. These give free sight in all directions and ample light.

The interior arrangement is one for convenience. Front entrance is gained through a large reception hall with semi-open stairway and arched entrance to large living room. This feature has proven popular, as it can be used for one room and still retain the convenience of two.

The kitchen has proved attractive to busy housewives. A rear entrance leads to the back porch, while the grade entrance at the side leads to the out-

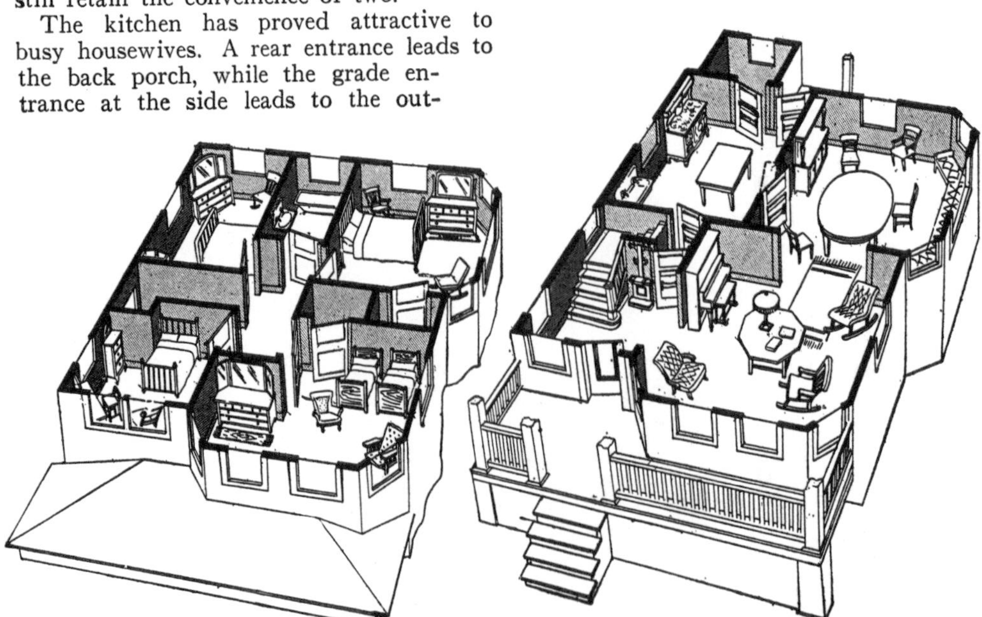

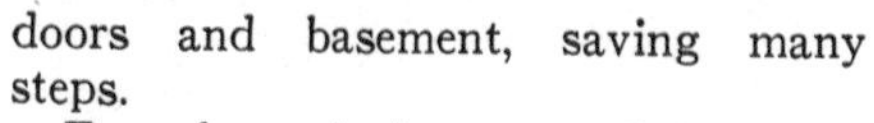

doors and basement, saving many steps.

Four large bedrooms and bath are arranged on the second floor—plenty of light in all. All exterior walls of siding. Beautiful Colonial columns support porch roof and a three-quarter length glass door adds greatly to the appearance. The Charleston is a good, substantial, roomy home.

Owners of the Aladdin Charleston home claim to save between $300 and $400 by building the Aladdin way.

This is due to the Aladdin Readi-cut system. All the material is cut to fit in the mills and reaches you ready to be nailed in place. In this way you pay for no waste of lumber or labor—you pay for the material that is used and no more.

From careful investigation it is estimated that the average waste of good lumber when building the old-fashioned way is between 18% and 25%. Do you care to pay big prices for lumber that is wasted?

See Terms on page 2 and General Specifications on pages 12 and 13.

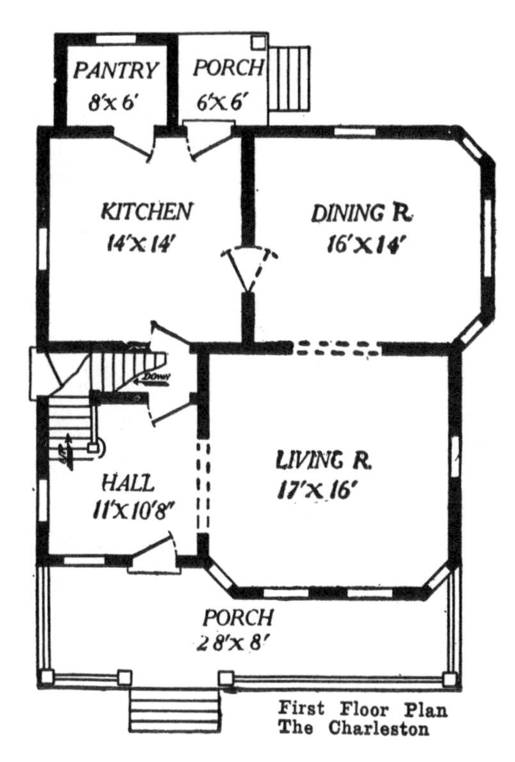

First Floor Plan
The Charleston

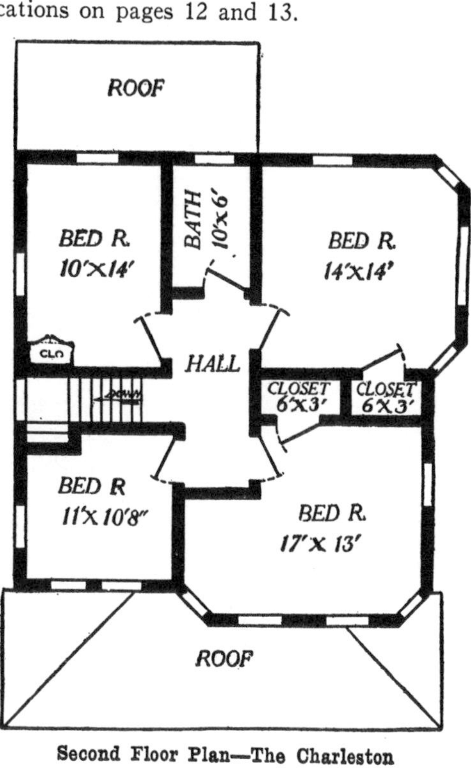

Second Floor Plan—The Charleston

The Richmond

MANY things distinguish the Richmond and set it apart from most homes. It's human nature to want things just a little different from the average, or ordinary. And to one who really seeks originality, dignity and, withal, convenience, the Richmond will have a strong appeal.

An impression of dignity is first gained by the colonnade. Extra large Colonial columns excellently spaced support the expansive roof and give balance to the front elevation. Four windows in a single group compensate for the shadows thrown by the main roof, and these windows make the living room very light indeed. Two groups of triple windows in the dormer serve the double purpose of embellishing the roof and making an exceptionally interesting bedroom on the second floor. Shingled walls and well balanced eaves are worthy your notice. A beautiful front door opens into reception hall with open stairway and an arch leads into a 14x18 foot living room. A cosy little den, or children's room is recessed back of the stairway. Another arch separates the dining room, which is 12x16 feet in size Cellar entrance and pantry lead from the kitchen. The second story has five good bedrooms, bath and closets. The Richmond will meet every wish for the comfort and pleasure of a large family and will effect a saving of nearly $1,500 to the builder, compared with usual construction costs.

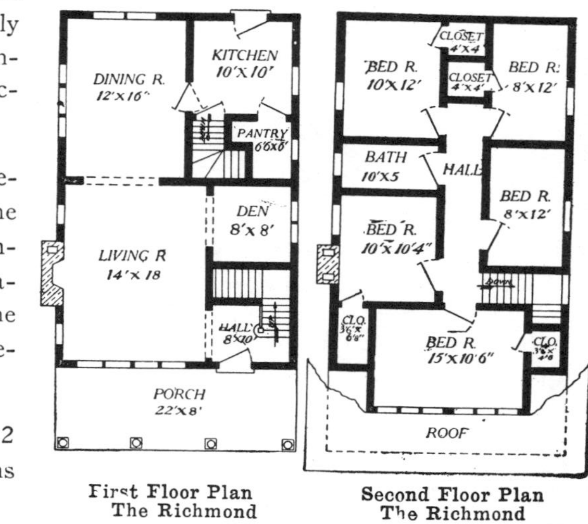

Send for complete detailed specifications on the Richmond. This list includes every piece of material entering into the Richmond, giving full description of each.

See Terms on page 2 and General Specifications on pages 12 and 13.

The Richmond

$1,396.50

Price, $1,470.00
Cash discount, 5%
Net price, $1,396.50

DINING R. 12'x16' · KITCHEN 10'x10' · PANTRY 6'6x6' · LIVING R 14'x18 · DEN 8'x8' · HALL 8'x10' · PORCH 22'x8'

First Floor Plan
The Richmond

BED R. 10'x12' · CLOSET 4'x4' · CLOSET 4'x4' · BED R. 8'x12' · BATH 10'x5 · HALL · BED R. 8'x12' · BED R. 10'x10'4" · CLO. · BED R. 15'x10'6" · CLO. · ROOF

Second Floor Plan
The Richmond

DID you ever really consider the wonderful difference in the meaning of the words house and home?

A house is a structure to live in.

Home—the dearest place on earth—is that structure that is a part of you—made so by its association with your family, their joys and sorrows, their hopes, aspirations, and fears. It is a refuge from the trials and struggles of the outer world. It is a visible expression of yourself, your tastes and character.

SERVICE!—that golden touch which changes the ordinary into the artistic.—It is that which is not bounded by the sale, but is added to complete or round out the transaction.

Aladdin's interest does not stop when the order has been received—but ever bearing in mind the many nice discriminations to be made in the locating, adorning, and surrounding of the home, the Department of Service was early established—to advise, direct or take full charge, as the home builders may desire, of this part of home making. As we have so often said, it is the use of such skill that changes a place to stay,—a *house,* to the dearest place on earth, a HOME.

Perhaps you find it difficult to express your tastes, as you feel them, when it comes to the arrangement, furnishing, and decoration of your home. You may not be sure of yourself. Right there is where our Department of Service can help.

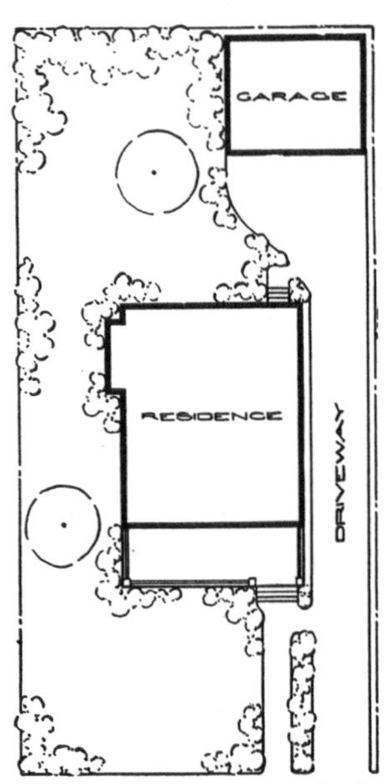

Example of Plan Furnished by Landscape Branch

This department is in the hands of people trained in the planning and arrangement of artistic exterior and interior effects for the home—design, decoration, landscaping, etc. It is organized and maintained for a single purpose—to serve our customers. There is no charge for this service.

If you have a general idea of color in the exterior painting plan that you would like to follow, let the service department work out the details. In the interior finish and wall colors you may either put the responsibility entirely up to the department, or by suggesting general preferences, it will work to your suggestions and carry out the details.

By furnishing the department with the size of your grounds, sketches will be worked out for attractive planting of shrubberies, plants, trees, etc., with lists of seeds and vines.

In fact, the Department of Service will help to make your Aladdin house *home,* in every sense possible.

In seeking this service you have only to address the Department of Service, care of this company. The service this company renders its customers in decoration and planting would cost from fifty dollars to five hundred dollars if you consulted the average landscape architect. It is but one of the links in the chain that forms such a close bond between our customers and us.

The Passing of the Pantry

Of the many conveniences efficiency has bestowed upon the housewife, the greatest and perhaps the most noticeable is the kitchen cabinet or kitchenette which replaces the old pantry. The majority of us, no doubt, can remember the old-fashioned pantry in which was stored a host of things—potatoes for the winter, preserves, fruits, barrels of flour, ice-chest, table leaves, brooms, etc.,—in fact, the pantry was a sort of catch-all —a rendezvous for a large variety of articles. At times, it was so overcrowded as to make it difficult to get thru the door.

But when efficiency entered, she swept aside the old-fashioned pantry with its multitude of things, and in its place arose the bright, sanitary and convenient kitchenette, a boon to the housewife and to sanitation.

The new and modern kitchenette accomplishes fully as much, if not more, than the old pantry did. It is convenient and sanitary, takes up less space than the pantry and saves the housewife hundreds of steps each day. No longer is it necessary for her to bring supplies back and forth from the pantry to the kitchen table. She may now sit at her cabinet with its work table and have at her finger's end the materials for a meal, as there is place for all necessary utensils and raw materials, such as flour, sugar, tea and coffee, spices, canned goods, bread-box, etc. And isn't the kitchen, rather than the pantry, the proper place for the preparation of meals?

Therefore, the majority of efficient housewives of today object to the annexation of a pantry to their kitchens, preferring the advantageous kitchenette in its stead.

Thus, efficiency has completely eliminated the old-fashioned pantry and has placed before the housewife a most commendable substitute—the modern kitchenette.

Aladdin kitchens are planned expressly for efficiency and step-saving.

Lot Sizes for Aladdin Houses

In order to assist you in selecting a home of proper size for your building lot, we have tabulated below a list of Aladdin Houses and size of lots necessary for each. This tabulation is given for the assistance of those who intend building on narrow lots in localities where ground space is costly.

Of course, you understand, a wider lot in each case would be more desirable, as it would show the home to better advantage and provide space for lawns, etc.

The following size lots will accommodate the style houses listed:

22-FOOT LOT

	Page
Tucson	57
Selwyn, No. 1	82
Erie, No 1	82

24-FOOT LOT

	Page
Finley	56
Chester	75

26-FOOT LOT

	Page
Venus, No. 1	40
Yale	28
Herford	32
Rodney, No 1	35
New Eden	44
Selwyn, No. 2	82
Erie, No. 2	82
Leota	95

28-FOOT LOT

	Page
Raymond	15
Venus, No. 2	40
Roseland	17
Princeton, No. 1	41
Stanhope, No. 1	72-73
Elliott	89
Dexter	89
Devon	90
Beverly	91
Standard	96-97
Thelma	98

30-FOOT LOT

	Page
Duplex	90
Richmond	66-67
Dresden	26-27
Wenonah	81
Suburban	34
Rodney, No. 2	35
Warren	85
Princeton, No. 2	41
Virginia	42-43
Hudson	46-47
Boulevard	51
Hamilton	58

32-FOOT LOT

	Page
Georgia, No. 1	92-93
Sheridan, No. 1	54-55
Rochester	37
Stanhope, No. 2	72-73
Detroit	74

36-FOOT LOT

	Page
Michigan	88
Putnam	91
Wilmont	18
Carolina	19
Sheridan, No. 2	54-55
Winthrop	63
Georgia, No. 2	92-93
Cadillac	94

40-FOOT LOT

	Page
Maples	16
Sheffield	36
Castle	38
Marsden	39
Sunshine	50
Gretna	59
Pomona	60-61
Edison	62
Franklin	80
Charleston	64-65
Plymouth	99

42-FOOT LOT

	Page
Merrill	78

44-FOOT LOT

	Page
Burbank	83
Florence	84

Interior Doors and Lock Set Trimmings

Furnished with Every Aladdin Home

HERE are some of the many beautiful details that are to be found in Aladdin Homes.

On careful inspection you will find that money cannot buy a better quality. Fir is distinguished for the wonderfully silky texture and softness of grain. You will never find two panels of the same design of grain and each one is an interesting study in itself.

The lock set trimmings for the interior doors are of the richest finished brushed brass.

The design on the escutcheon is an oak leaf pattern that stands in relief on the frosted background.

This beautiful lock set is made exclusively for Aladdin Houses.

The Aladdin Fir Door

THIS beautiful perfect grain door with two panels and the five cross panel type door are furnished for every Aladdin House. A real hardwood, but softer than oak or birch. Hard enough to take a hardwood polish, but soft enough to work easily. Aladdin Houses are finished better than most new houses in your neighborhood. We guarantee all your inside finish to be of exactly the same high-class material that this picture was taken from—clear lumber, beautiful grain—the best obtainable. Any stain furnished.

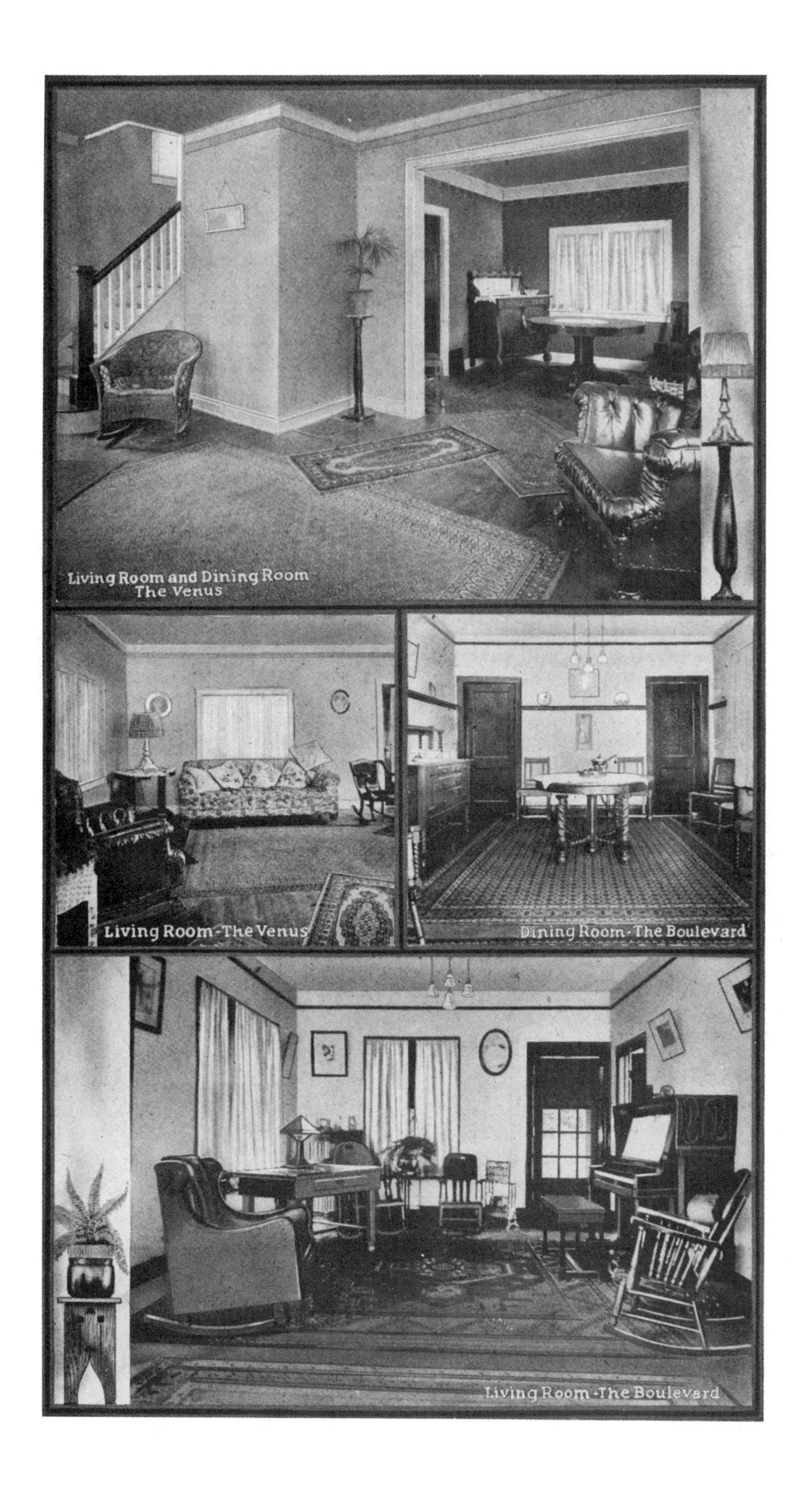

Living Room and Dining Room
The Venus

Living Room - The Venus

Dining Room - The Boulevard

Living Room - The Boulevard

The Stanhope $697.30

Price, Size No. 1, $734.00
Cash discount, 5%
Net price, $697.30

ARE you not pleased with the Stanhope? Can you conceive how with straight architectural lines any more pleasing or substantial style of construction could have been worked out? Notice what a strong yet artistic appearance is given the entire front by the heavy porch pedestals, square porch columns and porch rail.

How in keeping are the small lights in bungalow door and the upper divided lights in all windows. And when it comes to interior plan, it would be very difficult to work out a more convenient arrangement. The wide arch between living and dining rooms gives an appearance of one large room.

The double action door leading to a kitchen large enough, yet none too large, completes the living part of this compact, cosy home. Three well lighted, suitable sized bedrooms give as much sleeping room as is frequently found in a much larger home. For any one desiring a six-room modern house all on one floor, the Stanhope is a great favorite. The Aladdin readi-cut system of construction offers you a big saving on this home. You are now able to dodge the high cost of building because you pay for no waste of materials or labor in erecting an Aladdin. Match this against the excessive cost of waste in building on the old-fashioned method. Then compare market prices with Aladdin prices and you will realize the big advantage offered you in the Aladdin readi-cut system. It is estimated that 18% of the materials are wasted in building on the saw-measure-on-the-ground method. This means $18 out of every $100 is paid for waste actually lost! The Aladdin system has reduced this waste to less than 2%—put the $18.00 in your pocket. Can you afford to build on any other plan? Do you care to make this saving? Ask us for names of customers—let them tell you in their own words. There are many owners of the Aladdin Stanhope throughout the country. Probably there is one near you. We will send you names of owners—you can pay them a visit and inspect their home and material. Study General Specifications on pages 12 and 13. Complete detail specifications will be sent you upon request. See Terms on page 2.

Floor Plan
The Stanhope No. 1

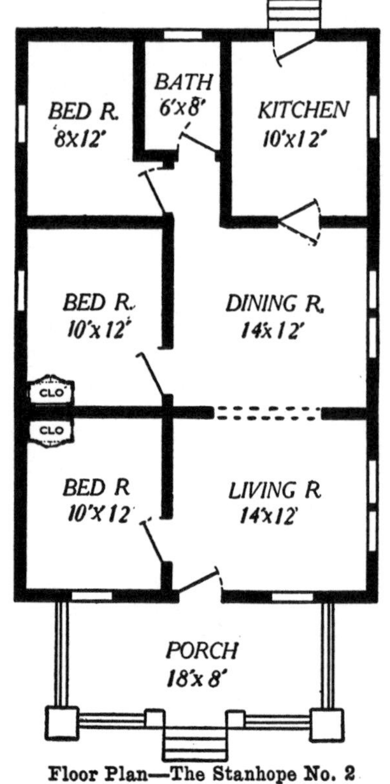

Floor Plan—The Stanhope No. 2

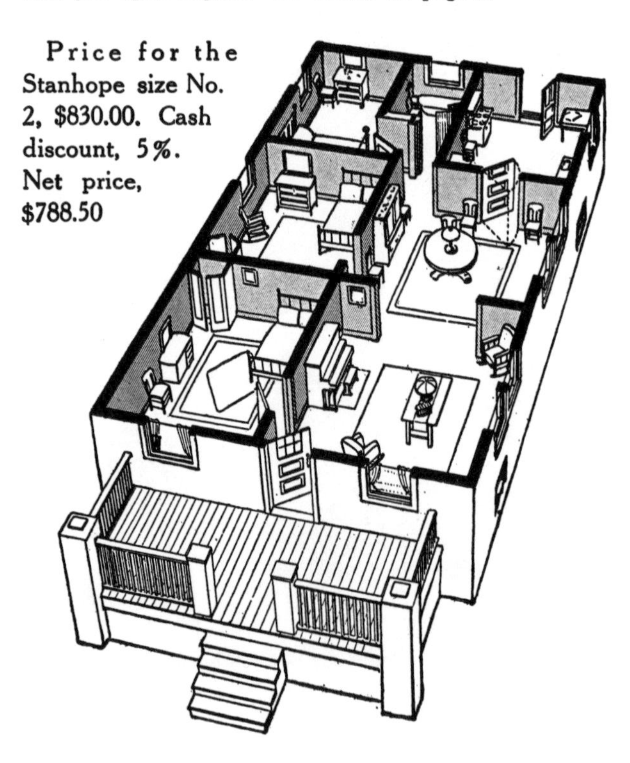

Price for the Stanhope size No. 2, $830.00. Cash discount, 5%. Net price, $788.50

The Stanhope

The Detroit $989.90

Price, $1,042.00
Cash discount, 5%
Net price, $989.90

A N enthusiastic owner of this attractive semi-bungalow wrote saying: "The more I see the Detroit and the longer we live in it, the greater becomes our love for it. After a year, we cannot suggest how your architects could make it more attractive or your designers improve the arrangement. This I believe you will admit is exceptional because usually after giving a house that most sure test of actually living in it, you have some improvement or changes you would make. We have none."

Who will not agree that actually living in a house *is* the best test? We believe that the longer you study the design and arrangement of the Detroit, the more fully you will realize why this owner has no improvements to suggest. Without being gaudy it is attractive, without being elaborate it is ample. No attempt has been made to embellish, yet you could not add anything without really destroying—in short the Detroit seems to stand complete—with nothing to add or leave off.

Notice how the porch extending the entire width of the house has been made not a seemingly attached part, but a real part by carrying over the main roof lines, while the double porch columns seem to give just the right stability for this style of construction. Artistic grouping of different style windows; open cornice, exposed rafters, straight line dormer, and an especially artistic porch rail construction seem to leave nothing to be desired.

In interior arrangement the Detroit is equally pleasing. (See interior illustration on page 45). The pleasant living room has opening off from it at the left, the downstairs sleeping room for those who wish, or the den or library for those that desire only sleeping rooms on the second floor. The broad archway gives easy access to the well-lighted dining room. Notice the combination of kitchen exit, basement and grade entrance. Compact, convenient and protected. The well-lighted kitchen with abundant wall space is especially pleasing to the housewife. Our attractive semi-open stairs lead to a central hall on second floor from which open the sleeping rooms and bath. Notice the size of the bedrooms — each of which has a large clothes closet. After in your imagination you have inspected the interior with our beautifully grained knotless fir finish, and again studied the artistic exterior, we believe you will agree with the many delighted Detroit owners. Complete detailed specifications, itemizing in full the complete list of material, are on file in our offices. Also copies of plans used as basis for figuring costs of erection are printed in handy form. They will be sent to you upon request. See General Specifications pages 12 and 13. See Terms on page 2.

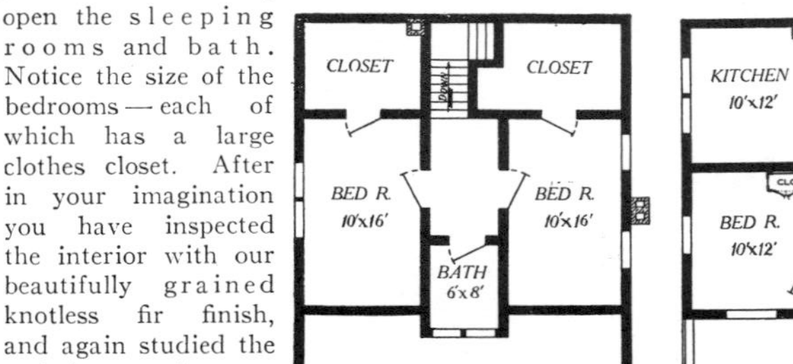

Second Floor Plan—The Detroit

First Floor Plan—The Detroit

The Chester $468.35

Price, $493.00
Cash discount, 5%
Net price, $468.35

BROWN shingles trimmed with white distinguish this little home from the ordinary looking cottages found in most communities. The Chester is a trim, neat, compact and pretty bungalow. Its five rooms are nicely arranged, its porch roomy and every room is well lighted. Note the spacious, airy living room that stretches the full width of the house and gives a view in both directions as well as in front. Arch separates dining room while two bedrooms and kitchen complete the home. You are privileged to choose any colors of paint and stain for shingles and trimming for the exterior, and you can have the most modern ideas worked out in your interior decorations with the wide variety of stains, varnishes and paints illustrated on our color cards. Most owners of the Chester write us about the pleasure they derived from erecting and completing it themselves. You can do this easily. With every Aladdin House we send complete instructions and illustrations for erecting. These instructions are so carefully written that anyone not a carpenter could easily understand them. It tells you how to start the work, kinds of material to use and in most cases gives illustrations of different stages in the erection. This information is sent to you in book form—over 100 pages—and includes information on every part of the erection from the digging of foundation to the time it is ready for occupancy.

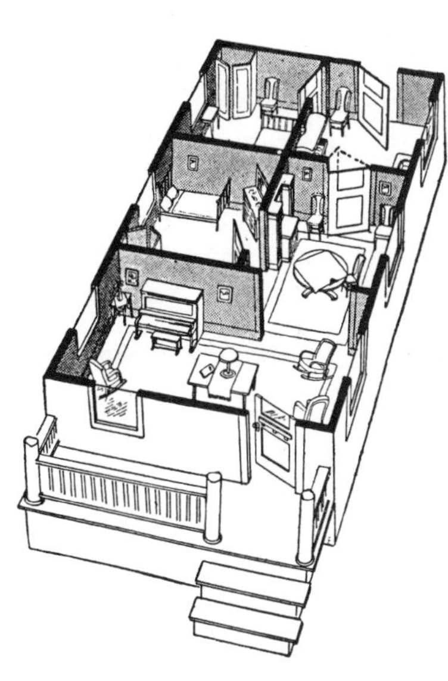

See Terms on page 2 and General Specifications on pages 12 and 13.

Barnard, N. Y.

"The Aladdin House is a rich man's house, but is in reach of every working man. I saved about $500 on my bungalow."

—L. L. Huyck.

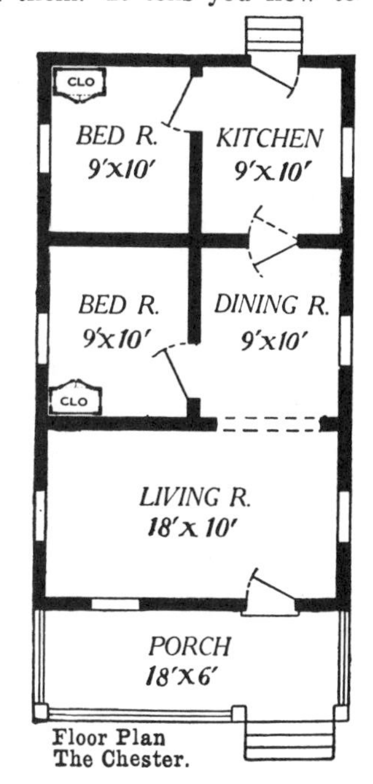

Floor Plan
The Chester.

The Strathmore $1,255.90

Price, $1,322.00
Cash discount, 5%
Net price, $1,255.90

THE Strathmore is different in design—it is a home of individual tastes. By noticing the photograph you will find that the special details are arranged in groups—double doors in front entrance, double windows balanced on each side, triple windows in dormer above. The double door feature owes its origin to architecture that was real popular in Colonial days. Today it is again coming into general favor in the largest and highest class homes on account of the pleasing effect it gives to both the interior and exterior of the home. The pergola porch at one side is another feature that pleases the average home-builder with modern ideas.

The interior arrangement will please you—notice the floor plan. The large living room is graced with a beautiful staircase. From the living room thru wide arch you enter the dining room with kitchen to the rear. One bedroom downstairs with three more and bath on the second floor make just an ideal home.

This design gives plenty of opportunity for home-loving folks to express personality and character in the decorations. This one pictured here was painted in white and trimmed in green. Excellent effects

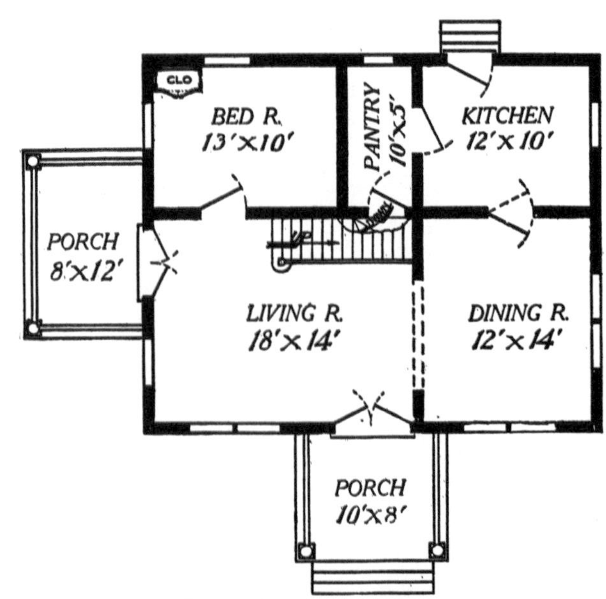

First Floor Plan—The Strathmore

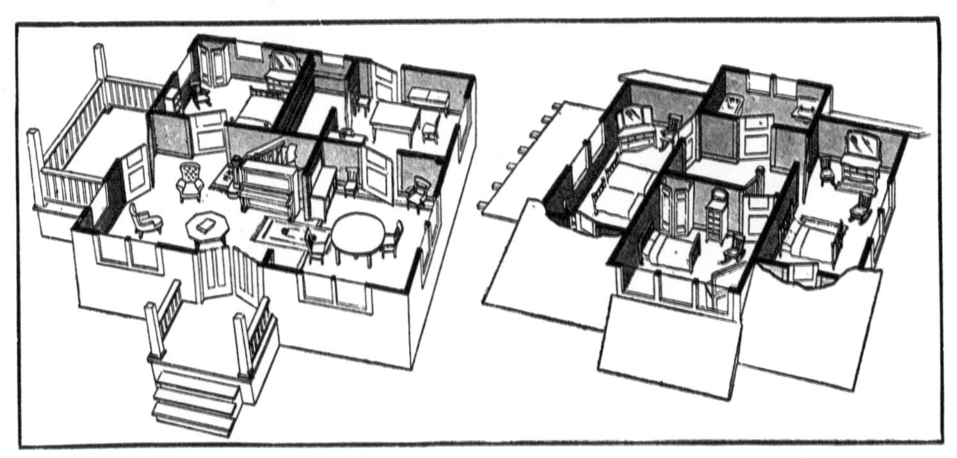

could be had by painting the house a lead gray or a yellow with white trim, or house painted in brown and trimmed with white. The living room—the one room that belongs to the entire family—could be papered or frescoed in deep brown with white ceiling. Space alongside of stairway would make a handsome setting for a davenport, wide seat or a piano. Of course, everyone has ideas for the decoration of their new home, and to help them, the Aladdin Department of Service will gladly send many more—and this free of charge. Let us help you plan this ideal home—the Strathmore—for your home.

By referring to page 70 you will note the style of interior door that is furnished for Aladdin Homes. These doors, as well as the interior finishing material for all Aladdin houses, are made from the most select of stock which is the beautifully grained Oregon Fir. Possibly no other wood is as attractively grained as Fir, and few other materials can be decorated as richly.

The Strathmore—Right Side

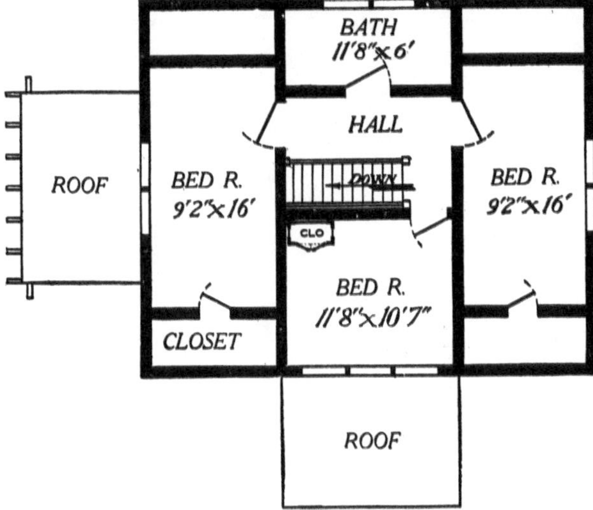

Second Floor Plan—The Strathmore

Many different stains can be used on Aladdin Fir with great success, among which are light and dark oak and dark mahogany.

Send for complete detailed specifications of the Strathmore which are sent upon request. A complete itemized list is given of everything entering into the Strathmore home.

See Terms on page 2 and General Specifications on pages 12 and 13.

The Merrill $898.70

Price, $946.00
Cash discount, 5%
Net price, $898.70

HAVE you ever seen a bungalow similar to The Merrill? Undoubtedly, you haven't, as it is a most recent Aladdin design—one built on both bungalow and Colonial lines.

The fact that this home is set close to the ground, built up but one story, finished with shingled sidewalls and heavy eaves supported by brackets, is an assurance of its bungalow nativity.

But here the designer sought a departure from the customary, and Colonial architectural lines were employed. Notice the front entrance with Colonial hood over front door. The side porch is also another Colonial feature which is a very desirable one.

The popularity of The Merrill is assured. Within sixty days' time after the plans were completed, and before it was given space in the Aladdin catalog, we had orders for thirty-two Merrill homes—a wonderful tribute to its practicability.

The interior of this home is one for convenience and attractiveness. The cased arch which makes a wide opening between living room and dining room, offers many opportunities for tasty decorations and arrangements. The living room on the front of the house is well lighted, has good wall space and offers the utmost in comfort to its occupants. The dining room is large, well arranged and offers the additional conveniences of the wide side porch. The plan shows three good-sized bedrooms, closets, bathroom and kitchen with cellar entrance.

See General Specifications on pages 12 and 13. Complete detail specifications for The Merrill will be sent on request. See Terms on page 2.

KITCHEN 12'6"x 8'
BATH 6'x 8'
CLO
BED R 12'x10'
PORCH 22'x 8'
DINING R. 16'x12'
BED R. 10'x10'
CL
LIVING R. 14'x14'
CL
BED R. 10'x10'
CEMENT PORCH

Floor Plan
The Merrill

Living Room-The Georgia No 2
Dining Room-The Georgia
Dining Room-The Kentucky
Living Room-The Kentucky

The Franklin $1,149.50

Price, $1,210.00
Cash discount, 5%
Net price, $1,149.50

ARE you pleased with the lines shown in the Franklin? This home has appealed to a great many. It was first erected in Bay City, the home of Aladdin and completed just in time to be classified in this book.

The excellent work of the designer is shown in the illustration. The keynote of the exterior plan is massiveness. Note the two large columns. They add strength to the front of the home and harmonize with the wide and heavy barge board. These columns are two foot square according to the plan.

Another feature that adds much to the attractiveness of the Franklin is the porch pedestals that carry the porch balusters, which you will note do not connect with the large supporting columns on the front. The pedestals—six in all—are a departure from the usual type of porch arrangement used in bungalow architecture tending to add much to the principal idea of the plan—strength.

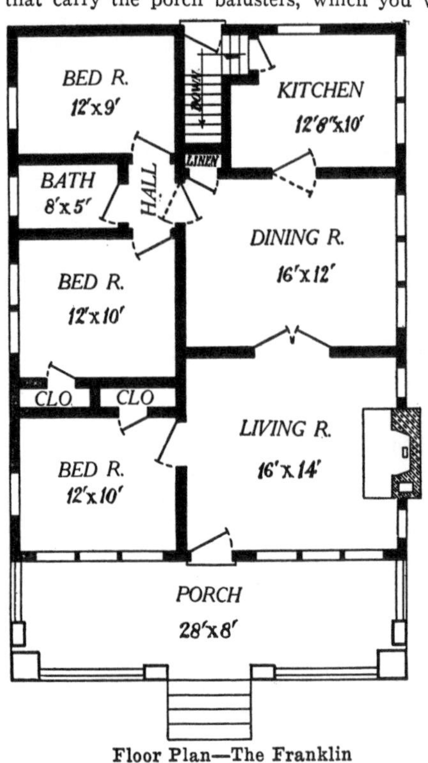

Floor Plan—The Franklin

Equal harmony is evident in the bay window in the front gable. This bay accommodates two single and one double casement windows.

And the Franklin interior has much to interest you. We ask that you notice the room arrangement. The living room and dining room will appeal to you. As the front door is swung open a feeling of comfort is evident. The wide living room offers many advantages in cosy and attractive arrangements and with the fireplace at one end gives all that can be desired in living room comfort.

The dining room is separated from the living room by an arch with double French doors. This feature is proving popular and besides this is a convenience on many occasions. Another point that we desire to call to the housewives' attention is the abundance of light furnished the kitchen by a double window on one side and single window on rear. Ideal efficiency arrangements of work tables and cabinets can here be secured.

The three good sized bedrooms are also well located. Each has plenty of light and wall space. The bathroom is situated off the hall at the rear.

Although the Franklin shown here is finished in stucco, it can be furnished with shingles or siding for sidewalls at the price quoted.

Send today for complete information on the Franklin, also detailed specifications. See General Specifications on pages 12 and 13 and Terms on page 2.

The Wenonah $1,444.00

Price, $1,520.00
Cash discount, 5%
Net price, $1,444.00

IMAGINE this house on your lot! Isn't it a beauty? It appeals to the lovers of practical architecture, as all traces of over-trimming are absent. The porch has much to do with the successful appearance of The Wenonah. The heavy columns with the roof projecting over half of the porch proper is pleasing, while the triple windows on each side of the second story give it harmony and individuality. An equally attractive interior arrangement is shown. Entrance hall, living room, dining room, and kitchen arranged on the first floor are furnished with plenty of light. The large living room is separated from dining room and entrance hall by wide arches. The four bedrooms and bath on the second floor are of good proportions, with ample closet room provided.

See General Specifications on pages 12 and 13. Complete detail specifications for the Wenonah will be sent on request. See Terms on page 2.

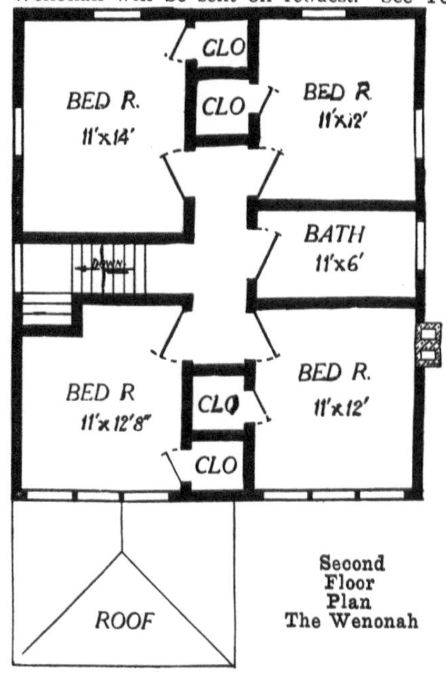

Second Floor Plan The Wenonah

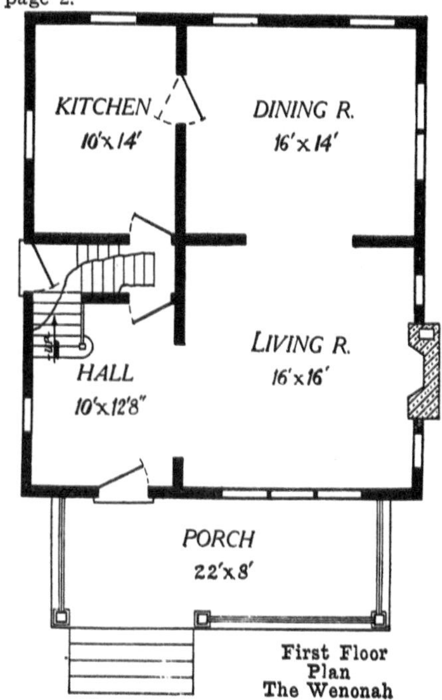

First Floor Plan The Wenonah

The Selwyn $318.25

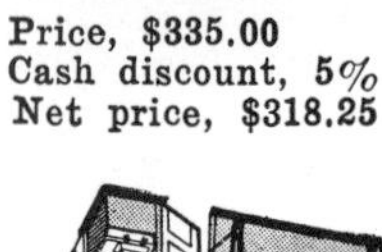

Price, $335.00
Cash discount, 5%
Net price, $318.25

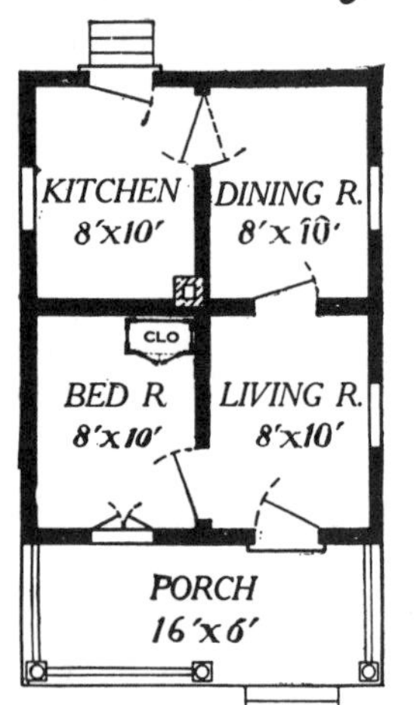

The Selwyn

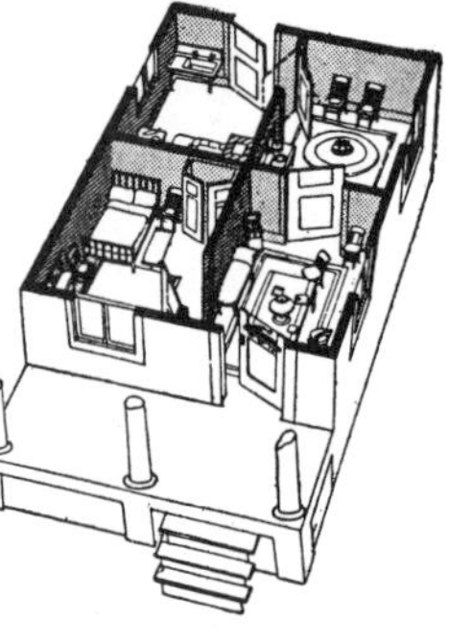

THE SELWYN! Isn't it a little jewel? Here is a real bargain. Here is a home that will be a great credit to you, to your building spot, to any location. How can we manufacture and sell this ideal home at this price? Here's the reason. Stop and think that your order is received today and enters the mill. Tomorrow it is rolled out of the mill yards and is on its way to you. Probably the same train has three or four more orders going in the same direction. Your house is but one of the many that leave the Aladdin mills each day, because Aladdin sells at wholesale prices and saves you the dealers' profits. Many a man of moderate means would like to own his little home, but the dealer's price, from $500 to $800, is too much, and it is difficult for him to engage carpenters. To all such the Aladdin Readi-Cut System is a blessing because they can build it themselves at a cost of simply their own time plus the cost of the material, or they can have it put up in a few days by day labor.

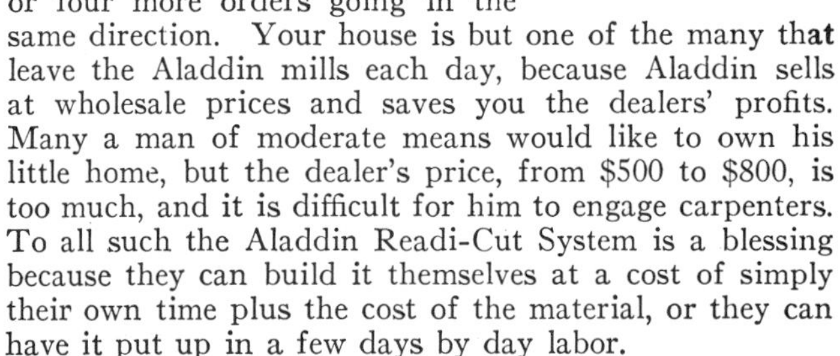

This little home of four rooms and attractive porch is a beauty. It is warm and strong—is built of the same high grade material as the larger Aladdin houses. Two men with no previous experience, following Aladdin's instructions, can erect this house in four days' time. You will take great pride in this Aladdin home—the Selwyn. The Selwyn and Erie will be furnished in size 20x24 feet instead of 16x20 feet as shown in these plans at an additional cost of $88.00 net.

See Terms on page 2 and General Specifications on pages 12 and 13.

The Erie

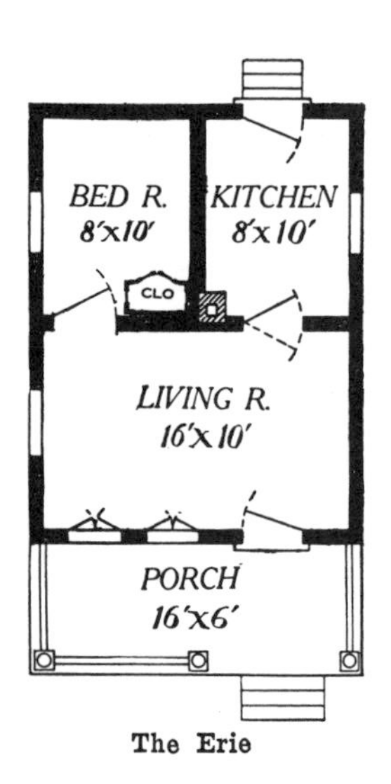

The Erie

The Erie is the same as the Selwyn, except it has a large 10x16 foot room across front of house. Price of the Erie is $329, cash discount 5%. Net price, $312.55.

See Terms on page 2 and General Specifications on pages 12 and 13.

The Burbank $879.70

Price, $926.00
Cash discount, 5%
Net price, $879.70

THIS picture tells a better story of Aladdin Golden Rule Service than anything that could be put into words. Our good friend stands on the porch, proud of the result of his industry, appreciative of the individuality and distinction of his home and enthusiastic in his praise of Aladdin materials and service.

In his choice of an Aladdin home, the extreme simplicity of outline of the Burbank appealed to him strongly and he saw the possibilities of shingled walls in a velvety brown, a soft green roof and an edging of pure white about the windows and eaves. The partial seclusion of the commodious porch with trailing vines took his fancy. But he is especially enthusiastic over the convenience of the rooms. Three fine bedrooms, a dining-room of unusual proportions and an excellent living-room, having grouped windows afford ample accommodations for a large family. **The kitchen is lighted by two windows, has cellar stairs and outside entrance.**

Beautifully finished woodwork and floors of the purest lumber complete a home to the last degree of satisfaction, and should you select the Burbank, or in fact any other Aladdin home, you can most certainly be assured of a result as splendid as is illustrated on this page. In further proof of this we will be glad to furnish you with the names of many Aladdin home owners who will vouch for their satisfaction, who will tell you of the money that they have saved and will even urge you to join the big Aladdin family.

General Specifications of the Burbank will be found on pages 12 and 13. Detailed specifications will be sent you upon request. See Terms on page 2.

KITCHEN 12'8"X8
BATH 8x6'
CLO
BED R. 10'x12'
DINING R. 12'X16'
BED R. 10'x10'
CLOS
CLOS
BED R. 10'x12'
LIVING R. 14'x14'
PORCH 22'x8'

Floor Plan
The Burbank

The Florence $858.80

Price, $904.00
Cash discount, 5%
Net price, $858.80

PRIDE of ownership! The very attitude of every member of the family in this picture denotes pleasure and satisfaction with their home: even to the extent of painting a small, neat name, that all who pass may know. The Florence is quite extraordinary in the almost universal appeal it has on observers. It is as clean in outline as a Greek temple and surely as pleasant to look upon as any home could be. To the lover of simplicity the Florence has a strong attraction, its well balanced and commodious porch, finely proportioned roof and dormer window, wide front windows and shingled gables all being in perfect harmony. And the material from which the whole is moulded is all as perfect as can be taken out of the forest. The owner has no lingering memories of paint covered defects to spoil his pride of ownership. The siding, the trim, the shingles, and the porch work are entirely free from knots or other defects.

The interior will appeal to the housewife. It rather surprises you to learn that there are three fine bedrooms, giving a large family ample accommodations. Living room is centrally located, which is much desired by many families. The bathroom is well placed, while the kitchen is made more roomy by a light pantry. Well placed cellar stairs give access to the basement from the kitchen. Beautiful floors and woodwork distinguish all Aladdin houses and of course give the finished effect to the Florence as to all our other designs. See Terms on page 2, and General Specifications on pages 12 and 13.

KITCHEN 9'x12'
PANT
BED R. 10'x10'
CLOS
CLOS
BED R. 12'x9'
BATH 8'x6'
HALL
DINING R. 12'x12'
LIVING R. 12'x14'
CLO
BED R. 12'x9'
PORCH 14'x8'

Floor Plan The Florence

The Warren $787.55

Price, $829.00
Cash discount, 5%
Net price, $787.55

STUDY the floor plan of the Warren and see if you can find an inch of waste space. It is the most practical of homes. There is much in the Warren that you cannot see at first glance. For instance, notice the short hallway inside the front door—just a dandy little place to hang the wraps of evening callers. The clothes closet built next to the hallway and opening into the bedroom is just ideal. Off the front hallway is the living room, and that it is well lighted by three windows at the front is noticed the moment you enter, and the wide arch dividing the living room from the dining room really makes them one big room. Through a door in the dining room you enter a hallway. It leads directly to the front bedroom, bathroom and back bedroom, separates living rooms from sleeping rooms so that neither one is disturbed by the other. The woodwork and floors can be finished any way you like for our beautiful Oregon Fir is unsurpassed by any kind of interior finish.

Both front and back bedrooms are compact. Now visit the home workshop—the kitchen. One can reach the dining room, basement or outdoors very easily. Now, have you found any waste space, or could you improve upon it in any way? The Warren has a great many friends. Will you be another?

"I saved four hundred and seventy-five dollars on my 'Warren,'" wrote an owner recently, "and to say that I am delighted with it is putting it mildly. My carpenter said the material was finer than we could get here at any price, and everything went together fine."

See Terms on page 2 and General Specifications on page 12 and 13.

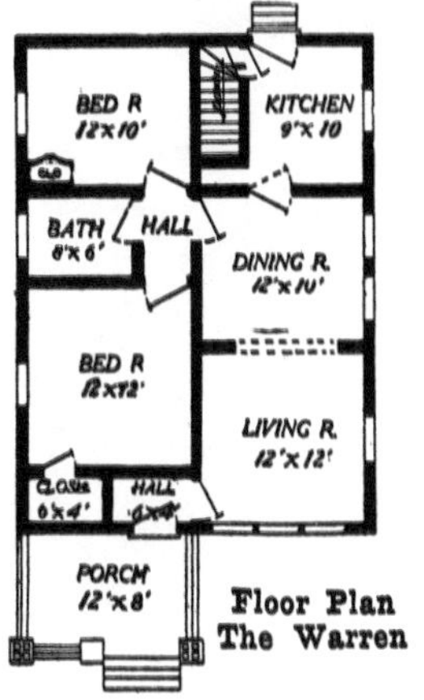

Floor Plan The Warren

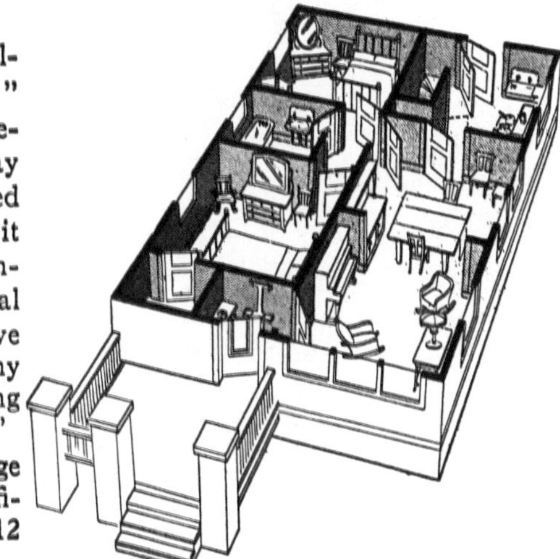

The La Salle

Price, $2,090.00
Cash discount, 5%
Net price, $1,985.50

$1,985.50

THE La Salle is a new design—one that was especially prepared by Aladdin's designers and erected for a well known citizen of Bay City, Michigan.

The architectural detail is purely Colonial. This is most evident in the window detail—plain sash below with divided lights above.

The dormers on the roof are in perfect harmony with the balance of the detail. The dormer windows as shown are of the casement type.

Most interesting of the exterior detail is the front entrance. The short terrace makes the five steps necessary to reach the semi-circle porch. Entrance detail shows no deviation from Colonial custom.

Sidelights on each side of the door, heavy brass door knocker and half glass door are purely Colonial.

There is much to interest you on the interior of the La Salle. The reception hall is the key to the entire home. It directly adjoins living room and dining room, connects with the den at the rear and the Colonial type staircase leads to the sleeping rooms on the second floor.

The long living room with fireplace suggests many attractive arrangements of period furniture and soft colors in decorations to secure the utmost in comfort and beauty.

The dining room is pleasant and well located at the right front corner of the home. It is separated from the kitchen by the butler's pantry. Note the back stairway to main stair landing.

Outside rear entrance leads to kitchen or basement.

The second floor plan shows four exceptionally large sized bedrooms, good closet space and bathroom.

Send for full information and detailed specifications for the La Salle. See General Specifications on pages 12 and 13 and Terms on page 2.

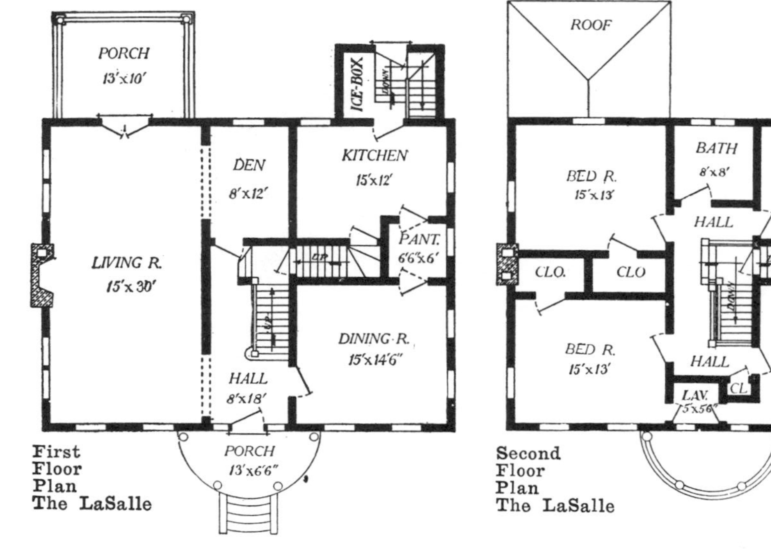

First Floor Plan The LaSalle

Second Floor Plan The LaSalle

The Michigan $896.80

Price, $944.00
Cash discount, 5%
Net price, $896.80

HERE is a model six-room dwelling which affords unusual value for the price. The interior rooms are arranged for convenience, ventilation and plenty of light. The vestibule opens direct into either the living room or dining room. The upstairs bedrooms are well lighted. A good sized porch with attractive turned pillars affords plenty of room for sitting out and enjoying pleasant weather. The Michigan is easily and economically heated, as it is practically square in proportions. Semi-open stairway in the living room with circle tread, and newel post and grade cellar entrance give a most modern interior. All doors are of our beautifully grained natural fir and can be finished in any way desired by the tastes of the owner.

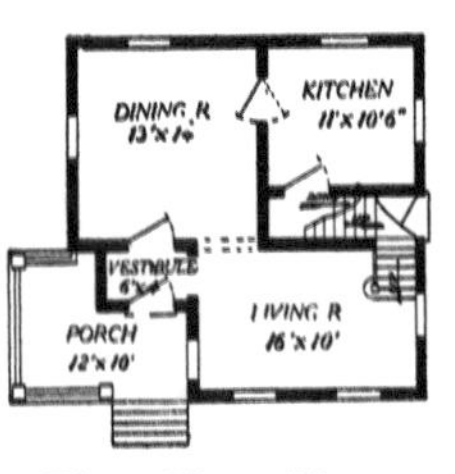

First Floor Plan The Michigan

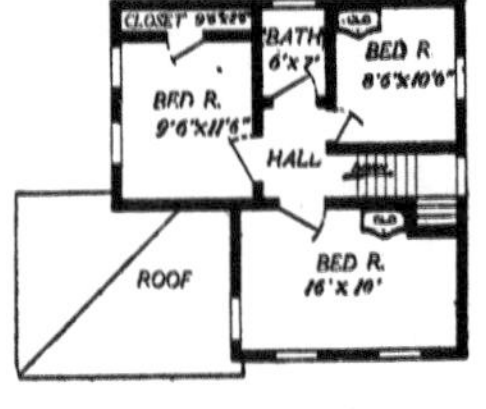

Second Floor Plan The Michigan

We have our "Michigan" completed, are living in it and are very much satisfied with everything. I know I saved between $800 and $900 and shall always be glad to recommend Aladdin houses. —Samuel G. Long.

See Terms on page 2 and General Specifications on pages 12 and 13.

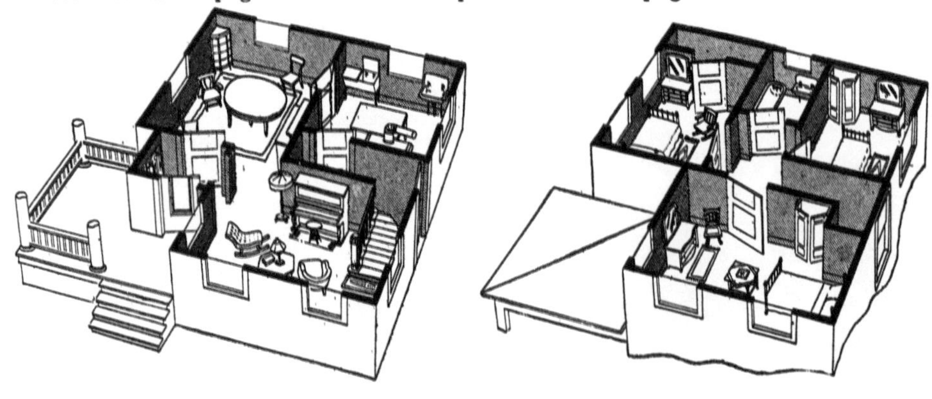

The Dexter

Two Apartment House

$1,597.90 Price, $1,682.00 Cash discount, 5% Net price, $1,597.90

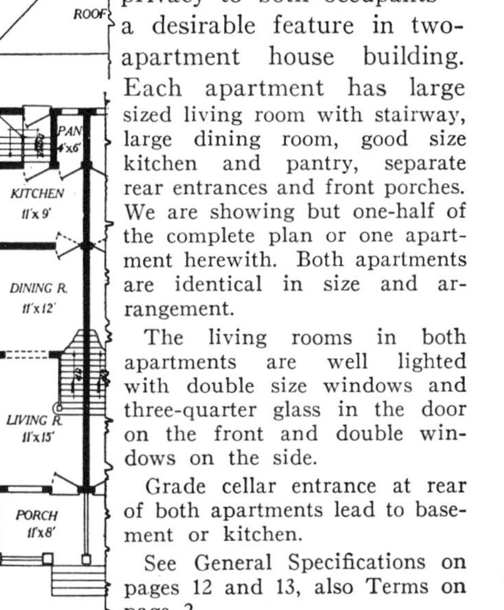

THE DEXTER apartment home has proven very popular among our customers who are building in the cities where ground space is sold at high rates and lots platted with narrow frontage.

The plan being but 22 feet wide over all contains excellent sized rooms very conveniently located. The arrangement is convenient and compact and insures privacy to both occupants—a desirable feature in two-apartment house building. Each apartment has large sized living room with stairway, large dining room, good size kitchen and pantry, separate rear entrances and front porches. We are showing but one-half of the complete plan or one apartment herewith. Both apartments are identical in size and arrangement.

The living rooms in both apartments are well lighted with double size windows and three-quarter glass in the door on the front and double windows on the side.

Grade cellar entrance at rear of both apartments lead to basement or kitchen.

See General Specifications on pages 12 and 13, also Terms on page 2.

The Elliott

$1,865.80 Price, $1,964.00 Cash discount, 5% Net price, $1,865.80

THE ELLIOTT was planned especially for a customer in the east who built in a high-class residential section. The illustration shown here does not portray it correctly as it presents a very pleasing appearance. Two features of the Elliott are the bay window in front and the return eaves on the second story. The bay window offers a cozy corner in the living room of both homes and adds greatly to the appearance of the exterior.

The Elliott is so planned as to make a complete apartment on each floor. The floor plan or room arrangement is ideal and proves very convenient to tenants. Living room and dining room, separated by cased arch, are both large and well lighted. The reception hall on the first floor serves both apartments.

The large kitchen is made more attractive by the addition of a cabinet. Three bedrooms and closets, bath, and grade entrance at rear complete the plan. Send for full detailed information. The second floor plan is an exact duplicate of the first floor plan. See pages 12 and 13, also page 2.

The Duplex

Two Apartment House

$1,267.30 Price, $1,334.00
Cash discount, 5%
Net price, $1,267.30

THE DUPLEX home shown here is one of the most desirable of two apartment plans. Each floor is complete with separate front and rear entrances. The floor plans give each occupant the utmost in privacy and convenience. Both floors contain living room, dining room, kitchen, two bedrooms, bathroom, pantry and porches. Send for full information on this home. The second floor plan is an exact duplicate of the first floor plan shown. See pages 12 and 13, also page 2.

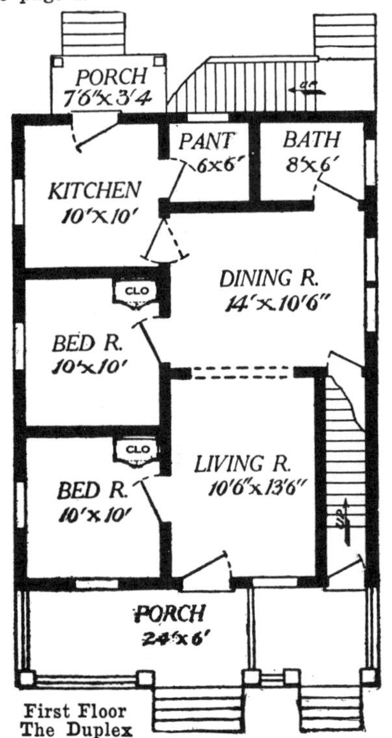

First Floor
The Duplex

The Devon

Two Apartment House

$1,696.70 Price, $1,786.00
Cash discount, 5%
Net price, $1,696.70

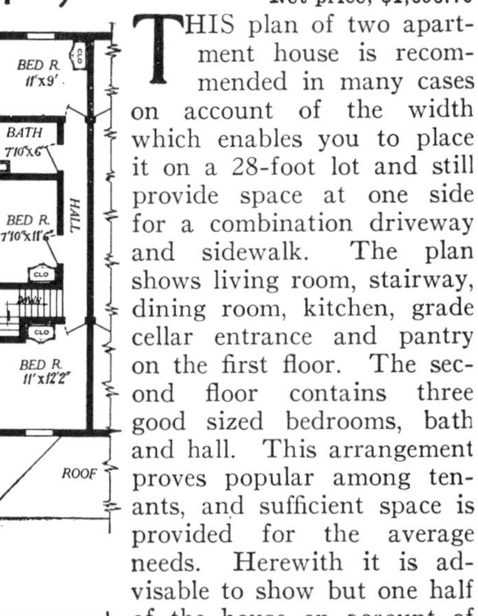

THIS plan of two apartment house is recommended in many cases on account of the width which enables you to place it on a 28-foot lot and still provide space at one side for a combination driveway and sidewalk. The plan shows living room, stairway, dining room, kitchen, grade cellar entrance and pantry on the first floor. The second floor contains three good sized bedrooms, bath and hall. This arrangement proves popular among tenants, and sufficient space is provided for the average needs. Herewith it is advisable to show but one half of the house on account of lack of space. The two plans here represent one apartment, the other which is not shown is identical in arrangement and size of rooms. Both apartments have front porch and front entrance and separate grade cellar entrances at the rear of the house. This apartment has proven an exceptionally popular seller and we have received many repeat orders after the first house was erected. Send for complete information on this house, also detailed specifications. We have shown only one side of floor plan as the opposite side is an exact duplicate. See General Specifications on pages 12 and 13. See Terms on page 2.

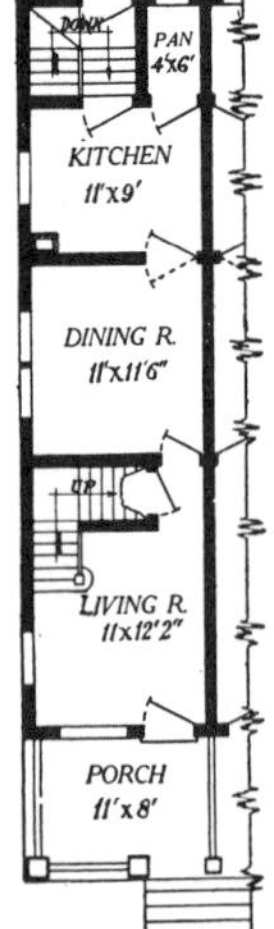

The Putnam

Two Apartment House

$1,795.50 Price, $1,890.00 Cash discount, 5% Net price, $1,795.50

THE PUTNAM apartment house is wider than the other two apartment houses we have listed but has proven very popular among our customers. One customer purchased two in the first order, and before they were finished had all of the four apartments leased to good tenants. Since the first two were completed we have received orders for four more. The Putnam provides larger rooms than the customary apartment house. Each plan has separate front porch, living room, dining room, kitchen, pantry and separate rear entrance on the first floor. Entrance to basement is directly off the kitchen. The staircase in the living room leads to the second floor, containing three large bedrooms, hall and bathroom.

On account of the lack of space we only show the first and second floor plan of one side, the opposite side being an exact duplicate. Detailed specifications will be sent on request. See Terms on page 2.

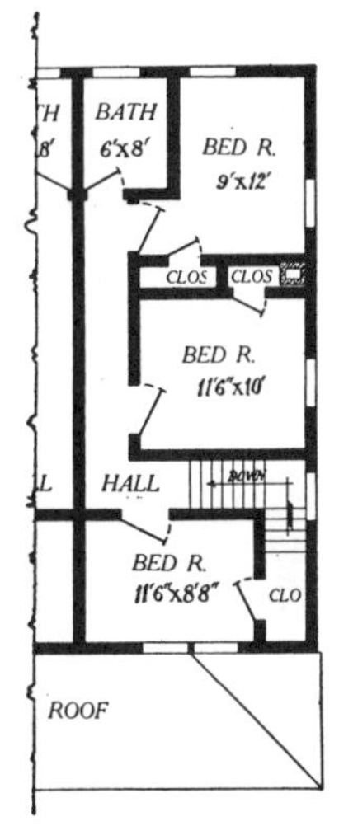

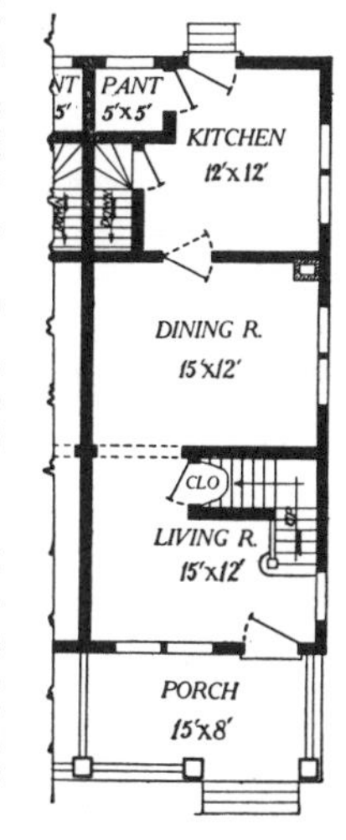

The Beverly

Two Apartment House

$1,688.15 Price, $1,777.00 Cash discount, 5% Net price, $1,688.15

THE BEVERLY makes a very attractive building. First story is sided while the second story is shingled. White, cream or gray on first story, brown shingle stain on second story with trim in white are the most popular schemes for exterior decoration. The plan of the Beverly shows a complete apartment on each floor, containing large size living room, dining room, kitchen, two bedrooms and bathroom. The side entrance serves both apartments, as it provides stairs that lead to basement or to second floor.

A 32-foot lot is necessary for the Beverly in order to provide combination driveway and sidewalk to rear of house. However, if these are not desired, it is possible to place the Beverly on a lot with 28 feet frontage. Send for complete information. The second floor is an exact duplicate of first floor. See General Specifications on pages 12 and 13, also Terms on page 2.

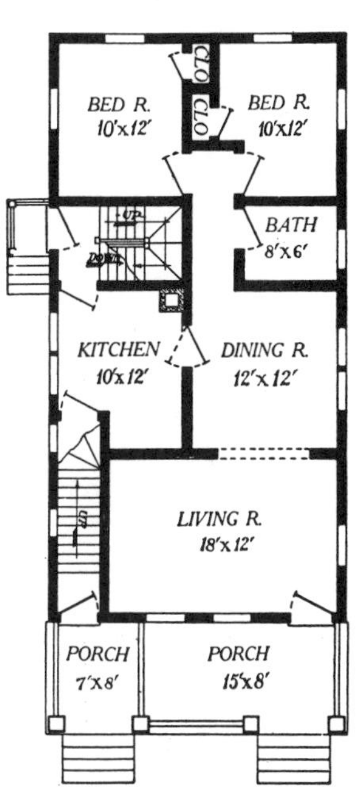

The Georgia

$848.35 Price, Size No. 1, $893.00
Cash discount, 5%
Net price, $848.35

Price, Size No. 2, $1,018.00
Cash discount, 5%
Net price, $967.10

THE Georgia presents a most unusual combination of true bungalow and two-story house. Excellent judgment by the designers gives it character and distinction. Observe the manner in which the exterior walls are divided by a belt, apparently cutting down the height, while the lower story is sided and the upper shingled. Timber brackets balance the overhanging roof, which is splendidly proportioned. The porch is unusual in shape and type, the longitudinal section being covered by a roof that partakes of the form and pitch of the main roof, but is relieved by the jutting gable covering that section of the porch floor projecting away from the front door. Square tapering columns supported by pedestals and joined by a well designed railing complete the porch.

Note the paired casement windows which afford excellent light to the interior. The upper gable windows are given an interesting touch by the little bracket-supported hoods. Living room, dining room, kitchen, grade cellar entrance, three bedrooms, bath and closets constitute a complete housekeeping establishment. And everything about this home gives a feeling of quality and refinement. The living room occupies one end of the home, having light from three sides. The handsome stained staircase leading to second floor is placed at the far end of the room. The wall space at the left of the stairway provides an excellent space for piano or large Davenport, leaving a wide stretch of space in the balance of the room, preventing a crowded appearance. The dining room directly adjoins the living room, being separated by a wide cased arch. You will be well pleased with the dining room, as it is of good size and made pleasant by the handsome grouped casement windows on two sides.

Right front view of Georgia

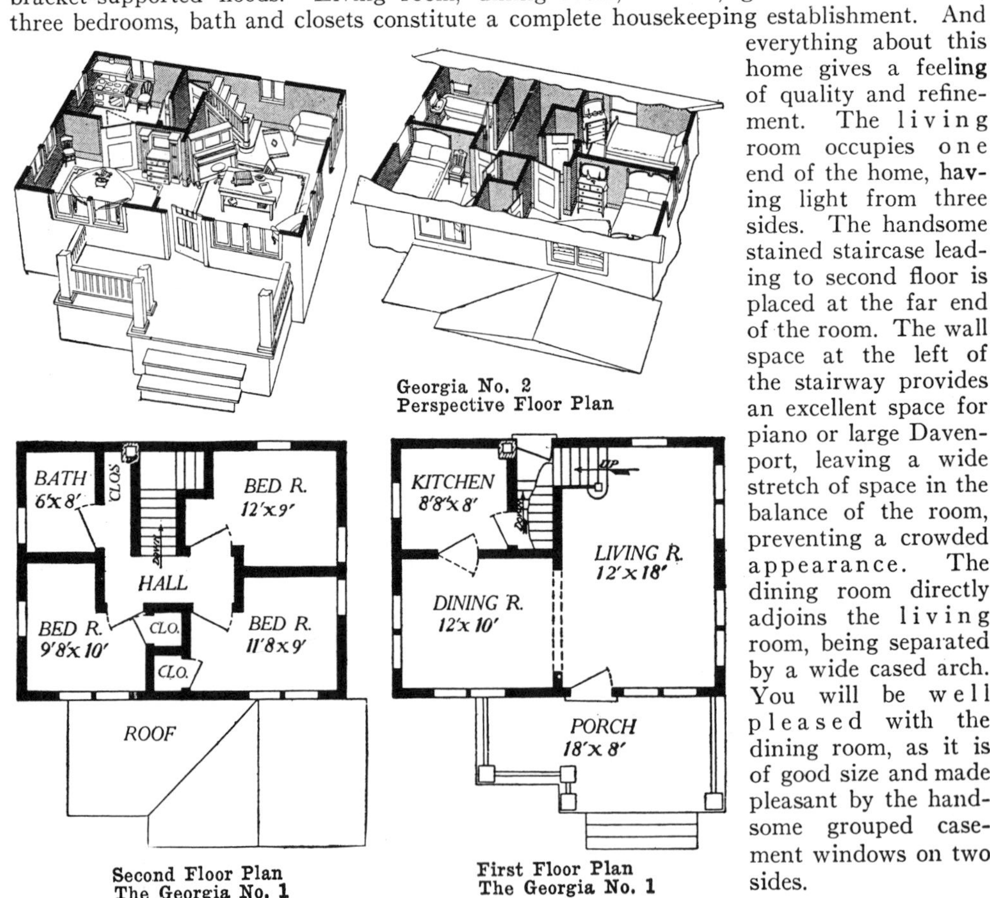

Georgia No. 2
Perspective Floor Plan

Second Floor Plan
The Georgia No. 1

First Floor Plan
The Georgia No. 1

The kitchen of the Georgia has attracted many housewives on account of its convenience. The grade cellar entrance makes it possible to enter the basement from the outside of the house without passing through the kitchen.

The pleasant and cozy rooms in the Georgia are made very attractive when finished in the beautiful Oregon Fir. This beautiful wood is furnished for interior finish in all Aladdin Homes. Photograph of the interior of the Georgia will be found on page 79.

One purchaser alone erected ten Georgias in 1915, an unusual tribute to its popularity.

See General Specifications on pages 12 and 13. Detail specifications for the Georgia will be sent on request. See Terms on page 2.

$967.10

Price, Size No. 2, $1,018.00
Cash discount, 5%
Net price, $967.10

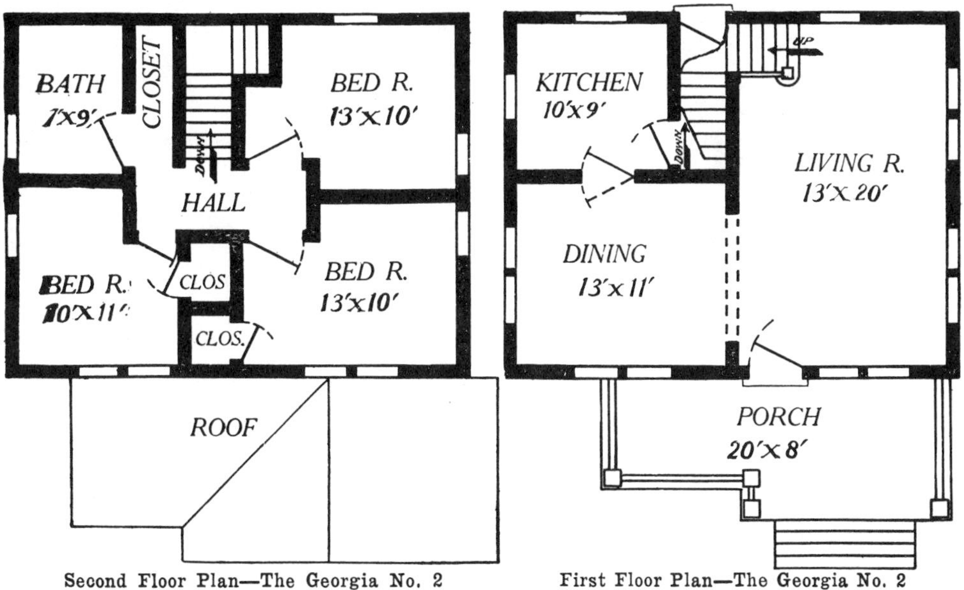

Second Floor Plan—The Georgia No. 2

First Floor Plan—The Georgia No. 2

The Cadillac $997.50

Price, $1,050.00
Cash discount, 5%
Net price, $997.50

THIS bungalow is worthy of consideration because it was planned by one of our superintendents for a home of his own. It was made exactly as he planned it to suit his experienced sense, fitness and ideas. Thus an individuality was brought about that attracts the attention of every passer-by.

It is a home that is pleasant and has an abundance of space within for comfortable living and would give to anyone that possessed it a great pride of ownership.

The exterior is artistic and pleasing to the eye. The broad sweep of the roof carried out over the porch adorned with a dormer, breaking the wide expanse, is perfect in proportion and balance. The square divided lights in the upper sash of the windows lend an added charm to the exterior.

The main floor comprises a large living room entered directly from the porch. Off of this is a spacious dining room and den. Attractive French glass doors enable the owner to combine these rooms in one. The fireplace shown in the floor plan could be built in the opposite end of the living room, if desired, or could be omitted entirely.

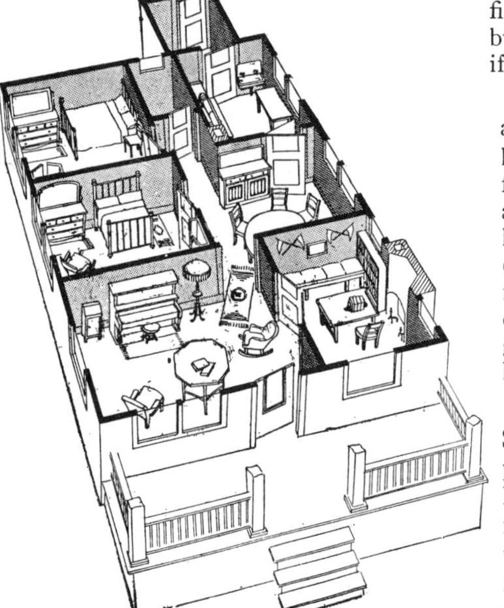

Two bedrooms furnished with closettes as well as bath and kitchen finish the floor plan. Directly at the rear of the kitchen is a very convenient and modern grade cellar entrance addition, giving access to the kitchen and cellar.

See General Specifications on pages 12 and 13. Detail specifications for The Cadillac will be sent upon request. See Terms on page 2.

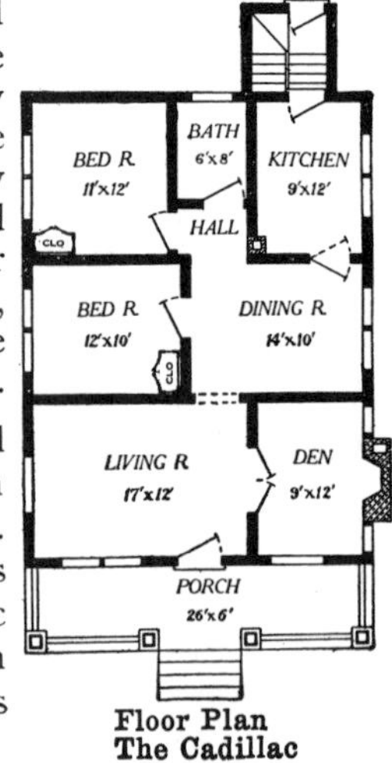

Floor Plan
The Cadillac

The Leota $475.00

Price, $500.00
Cash discount, 5%
Net price, $475.00

"CRAFTSMAN" front door, casement windows grouped in pairs and side walls shingled are the particular ideas moulded into The Leota. Another new thought is the side entrance to the porch. The porch posts should be very heavy and built of concrete as well as the porch floor. The interior arrangement is well illustrated by the floor plans shown below. This little gem of a bungalow will match, in both material and construction, homes of many times its cost. Beautifully grained interior wood work, frosted brass hardware fittings and the finest stains and varnishes to be bought combine to give you a most interesting bungalow. Note the casement windows with divided lights and exposed rafter ends. When erected this bungalow is worth very nearly two thousand dollars, without the lot. You'll like every feature of it. The Leota is built of the same materials and in identically the same way as the Aladdin house which was erected at the Panama-Pacific International Exposition, and which was awarded the highest prize by the International Jury of Awards. It is built of the same material and in identically the same way as the homes of the President and the other officers of The Aladdin Company. The same beautiful, clear and flawless lumber, high priced paints, stains, varnishes and hardware are furnished as in all Aladdin houses. While no cellar is shown under The Leota from which this picture is taken, you can of course have a full cellar, as in any other home.

KITCHEN 10'x 9'
BED R. 10'x 9'
DINING R. 10'x 9'
BED R. 10'x 9'
LIVING R. 20'x 10'
CONCRETE PORCH 16'x 6'

Floor Plan—The Leota

Remember, you can erect your own Aladdin home and save the cost of skilled labor. Hundreds of Aladdin customers have erected their Leota homes from the complete instructions for erection that are sent with every order. Ask for names of customers—let them tell you in their own words.

See General Specifications on pages 12 and 13. Detail specifications for The Leota will be sent on request. See Terms on page 2.

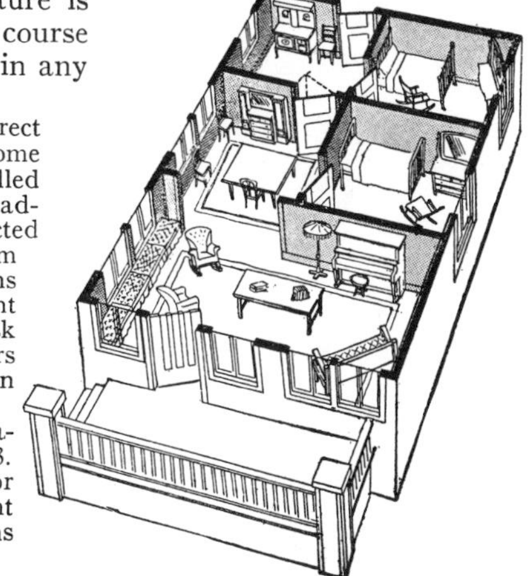

The Standard $1,187.50

Price, $1,250.00
Cash discount, 5%
Net price, $1,187.50

YOU will agree with Aladdin customers and owners of the Standard in their claim that "it is the best square type house ever offered to home builders." Greatest in amount of space, best in point of design, most convenient in arrangement, and all this at a price that is much lower than it would cost you if you were able to buy thru any other source. Notice the architectural detail under the eaves, porch, and the dormer.

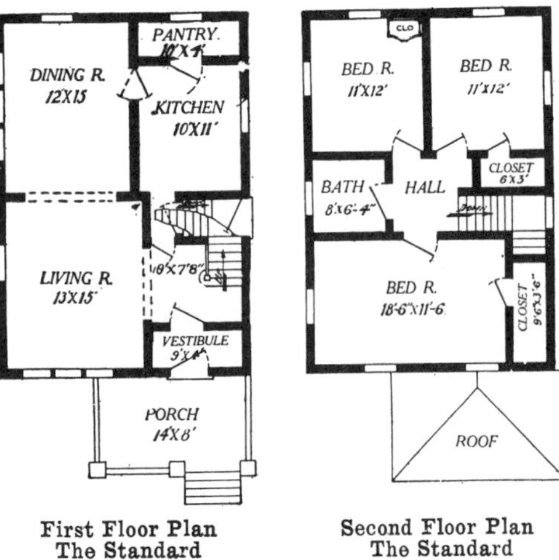

First Floor Plan
The Standard

Second Floor Plan
The Standard

Close inspection of the illustration gives many pleasant surprises. The scrolled brackets which are especially machined for the Standard, add a finished touch to the sweeping eaves. Possibly you have noticed that this has been carried out on all eaves—dormer and porch included. The broad belt is also used to advantage here.

The inside arrangement has appealed to many. Notice the vestibule entrance. This is a very useful feature in that it provides an excellent place for hanging wraps. Besides this, it is a valuable feature in cold weather. Thru the next

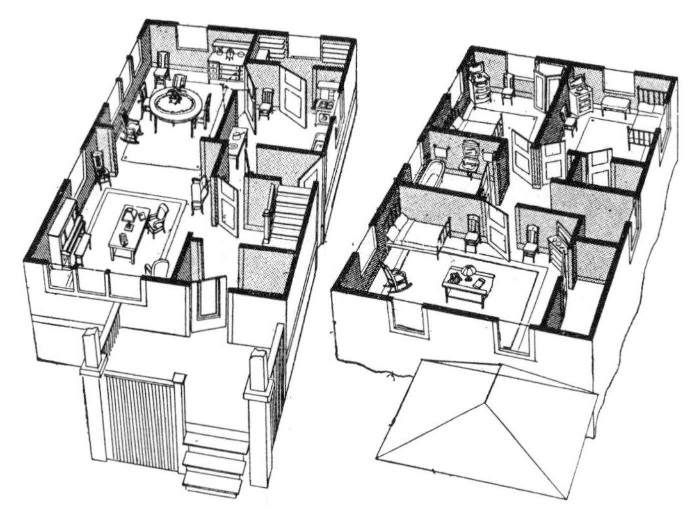

door we enter what might be called a reception hall and the impression is very pleasing indeed. The handsome exposed staircase can be beautifully stained and varnished and gives one an idea of the rich effect on the interior. You find that the living room and dining room are extra large—and that will suit you—roomy and especially well-lighted.

The kitchen in the Standard home invites efficiency methods. First, the size is ample for working to advantage. Second, no waste steps are necessary. Pantry at the rear is but a few steps away while the dining room but another few steps through double action door. Either the reception hall or the grade entrance leading to basement or outside may be reached directly, meaning a saving of time.

The second floor has model sleeping rooms and the arrangement with bath at the head of the hallway is perfect. Each of the three bedrooms shown on the plan are extra large and have excellent wall space for beds, dressers, etc. Two of the bedrooms have large closet space directly adjoining—the other bedroom is provided with the convenient Aladdin closette. For complete information on the closette refer to page 115. All ceilings in bedrooms are square and not hipped. You will be greatly pleased with your new home—The Standard.

See General Specifications, pages 12 and 13. Complete detail specifications for the Standard will be sent on request. See Terms on page 2.

Living Room—The Standard

The Thelma $495.90

Price, $522.00
Cash discount, 5%
Net price, $495.90

The Thelma seems to be really more than a home. It is really an additional member to the family that offers pleasure for the lonely, rest and comfort for the tired, and shelter when it's stormy.

Study the floor plan again. Imagine furniture, carpets and curtains in place, and a happy family seated comfortably in the living room or on the porch.

It would be hardly possible to get a better plan. The room arrangement is just right. Dining room, living room, kitchen and two bedrooms—and each with plenty of light. Note that both dining and living rooms have double windows facing the front.

The delightful exterior, the interior with its coziness and the low price quoted for the complete material are your assurances of the highest satisfaction.

If you decide *now,* one month from today you can be living in the Thelma.

See Terms on page 2 and General Specifications on pages 12 and 13.

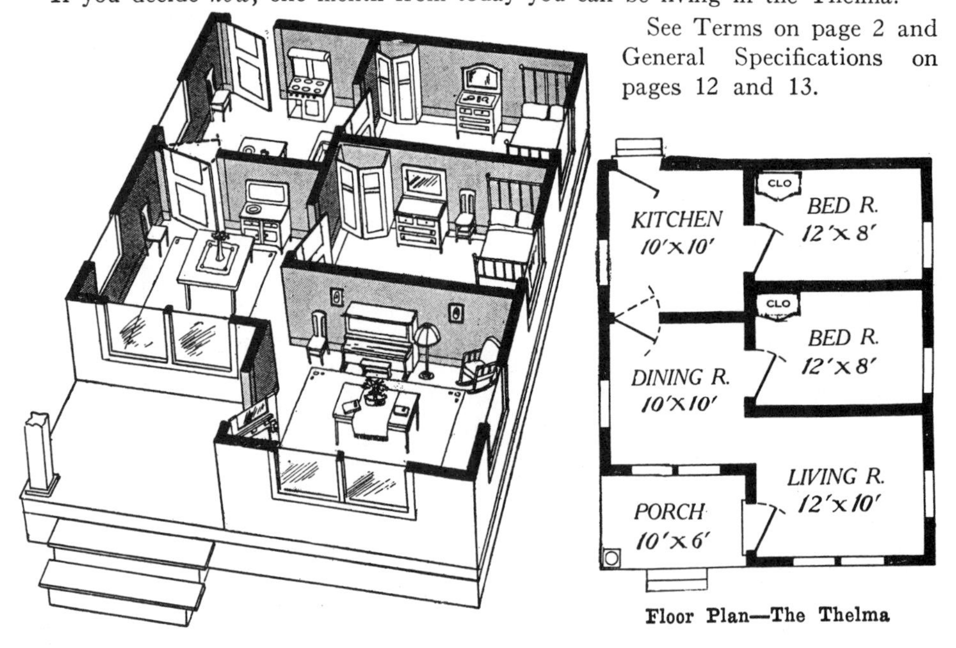

Floor Plan—The Thelma

The Plymouth $649.80

Price, $684.00
Cash discount, 5%
Net price, $649.80

SIMPLE square lines have been here transformed into a charming home. The plan is quite different from anything else shown in our book, yet the arrangement of rooms, convenience and access, one room with another, is excellent. Note that the entrance hall gives access to three different rooms and is but a step from the kitchen. The living room is separated from the dining room by the hall, with a vista of two arches. Light is admitted to hall by windows on each side of front door. Two bedrooms, bath and kitchen complete this snug design. The exterior is shingled, and shows very wide eaves with exposed rafters. Although the chimney is shown on the outside of the house, it can be placed in any part of the home.

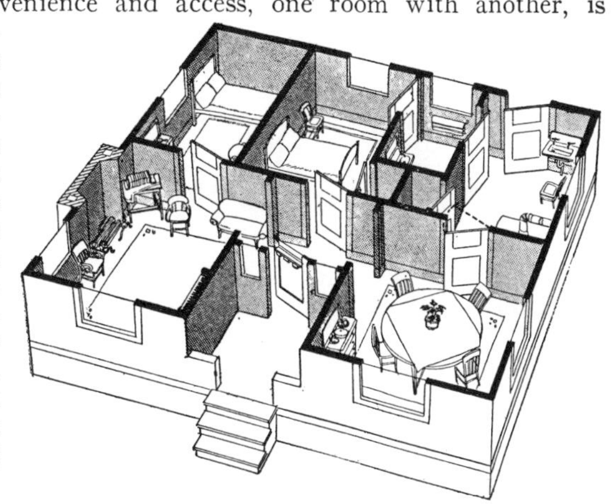

The most noticeable features to visitors of the Plymouth is the beautiful interior finish. When stained and oiled in the rich tones of oak the attractive grain in the fir finishing material contrasts handsomely with the delicate shades used for interior decoration. All the fir material used for interior finish in every Aladdin Home is carefully selected for the finest grain patterns.

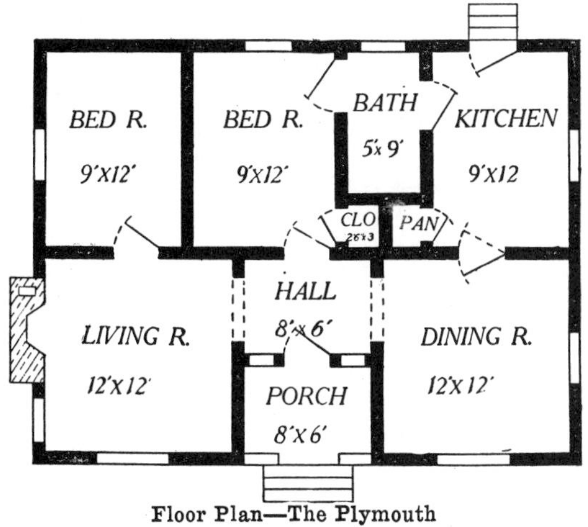

Floor Plan—The Plymouth

See General Specifications on pages 12 and 13. Detailed specifications of the Plymouth will be sent on request. See Terms on page 2.

Aladdin Readi-Cut Barns

THE word Aladdin means as much to barns as it does to homes. Aladdin barns are built for strength and durability. The quality of the material is far superior to that found in the average barn.

Each Aladdin Barn is very strongly constructed, in fact, stronger than it is usual to build barns of the same size erected by usual methods. The timber in every barn is heavier and stronger than it is really necessary to use in a building of the same size. We appreciate the great weight and strains that are put in farm barns at times, and each barn is constructed so as to stand a greater weight than it will ever be called upon to hold.

They are not only constructed of very heavy timber, but are braced and counter-braced wherever this bracing will increase the strength of the building.

Each barn has material cut to fit ready to nail in place the same as all our other regular dwellings and houses. In fact, they are better finished than it is usual to build ordinary barns throughout the country. All of the material is dressed so that the inside of each building presents a finished appearance and is not merely of rough unfinished lumber.

We furnish all the different kinds and sizes of nails required in the erection of the building; heavy barn door tracks and rollers for the large doors to slide upon; hinges and locks for the smaller doors. The windows have the glass already in them.

We will furnish any colors of paint that you may desire for the outside of the building, two coats; shingles or roofing, whichever you prefer, for the roof of the building.

We have quoted the prices on the barns so that you can purchase either the barn itself, or so that you can leave out the first and second floors and the stalls, or so that you can purchase the building with the first floor added, or with the second floor added, or with both floors added. We have also quoted the price separate on the stalls, so that you can add any number of stalls you desire with the building. For example, a gambrel roof barn, size 20x40 ft., without first or second floors or mangers, would cost $421.08. First floor furnished with the barn would cost $82.12 extra, or $503.20 for barn and first floor complete. For a gambrel barn, size 20x40 ft., with first and adding second floors and mangers, for two stalls the cost would be $550.70 complete.

Each barn as we furnish it, and as listed in the cost on the barns, will include a second floor at one end above the stalls. This second floor will be twelve feet long and the width of the end of the barn, and is always included in the first cost of the barn.

Many people prefer to purchase the barn without the first floor, which is really unnecessary in many cases, where hay and grain are intended to be stored into mows. Others prefer to put in either a part or the entire first floor in cement, so that we have quoted the price of the barn exclusive of both floors and stalls, and have listed separate the cost of each. This will enable you to purchase the barn itself and add either the first or second floor or any number of stalls desired.

Aladdin Special Barn $275.50

Price, $290.00
Cash discount, 5%
Net Price, $275.50

The Aladdin Special was built to meet the great demand for a barn large enough to shelter two or three horses with wagons, etc. Plenty of room on the first floor for three stalls, with a large mow on second floor for hay, straw and grain. At the price quoted, the second floor is included, but the first floor is omitted, as many owners prefer a cement or concrete first floor on account of the convenience in cleaning stalls, etc.

SPECIFICATIONS: Size, 16 x 24 ft. See Terms on page 2.

Sills, 6 x 6 in. Studding, 2 x 4 in. Rafters, 2 x 4 in. Second floor joists, 2 x 8 in. Siding, ⅞ in., matched; roof sheathing, 1 in., dressed. Flooring, second floor, 1-in. lumber. Shingles or roofing for roof. Large door, 8 ft. 4 in. x 9 ft. 6 in. Small door, 3 ft. 6 in. x 7 ft. 2 in. Windows, sliding sash, glass in place. Paints, any colors, two coats, outside. All hardware, nails, barn-door tracks, hinges. At the price quoted above, second floor is included. Add $39.42 to the above price for first floor of 2-in. planks, including first floor joists of 2 x 8 in.

The Gable Barn

THE Gambrel and Gable Roof Barns are here shown. The construction and material of both barns are exactly the same, the only difference being in size and design. These barns have given the greatest satisfaction and service on the western plains of Nebraska and Kansas, where they are subjected to the heaviest strains of wind and storms. This goes to prove the great strength and stability of the construction.

Gambrel and Gable Barn Specifications

Sills, 6 x 8 in.
Studding for the side walls and gables of barn, 2 x 6 in.
Rafters, 2 x 6 in.
Collar beams, 2 x 6 in.
Cross braces in outside walls, 2 x 6 in.
Anchor brace, 2 x 6 in.
Plates of top walls, doubled, 2 x 6 in.
First floor joist, 2 x 12 in.
First floor flooring, 2-in. plank.
Second floor joist, 2 x 8 in.
Second floor flooring, inch lumber.
Stall studding, 2 x 4's.
Stall siding, inch lumber, dressed.
Mangers, attached to stalls, inch lumber, dressed.
Feed boxes, inch lumber, dressed.
Roof sheathing, inch lumber, dressed.
Roofing or Cedar shingles for roof.
Siding, perpendicular barn boards or horizontal matched siding, whichever you prefer.
Windows, 18 x 24, glazed, glass measurement.
Doors, double and single.
Barn door tracks and rollers for sliding doors.
Hinges and locks for swinging doors.
All nails of various sizes for entire building.
Two coats of paint, any color desired for outside.
Complete instructions and illustrations for the erection.
Total height of side walls, 12 ft. gambrel, 15 ft. gable.

Below we have listed the prices for both designs, gambrel and gable roofs, with specifications that include either the gambrel or the gable design. The gambrel barn is illustrated at the bottom of the page.

Gambrel and Gable Barns

Height of Side Walls of Gambrel Barn is 12 feet 0 inches, and of Gable Barn is 15 feet 0 inches. Prices Given are for Either Style. Gable Roof Barn Illustrated on Following Page.

Size	Price Net Cash	First Floor Extra	Second Floor Extra	Stall with Manger Extra
16 x 24 ft.	$250.20	$39.42	$11.94	$5.50
20 x 30 ft.	339.90	61.60	23.46	5.50
20 x 40 ft.	421.08	82.12	36.50	5.50
20 x 50 ft.	502.92	102.67	49.54	5.50
20 x 60 ft.	584.76	123.20	62.58	5.50
20 x 70 ft.	666.60	143.73	75.62	5.50
20 x 80 ft.	748.44	164.27	88.67	5.50
20 x 90 ft.	831.60	184.80	101.71	5.50
20 x 100 ft.	912.45	205.33	114.75	5.50
24 x 30 ft.	386.10	73.92	28.15	5.50
24 x 40 ft.	476.85	98.56	43.79	5.50
24 x 50 ft.	569.25	123.20	59.43	5.50
24 x 60 ft.	660.00	147.91	75.07	5.50
30 x 40 ft.	561.00	123.20	54.74	5.50
30 x 50 ft.	666.60	154.00	80.81	5.50
30 x 60 ft.	770.55	184.80	106.87	5.50
30 x 70 ft.	874.50	215.60	132.94	5.50
30 x 80 ft.	980.10	246.40	159.01	5.50
30 x 90 ft.	1,084.87	277.20	173.19	5.50
30 x 100 ft.	1,189.98	308.00	199.26	5.50

Sovereign Summer Cottages

THE many pleasures and advantages of summer cottage life need no argument here. Thousands and thousands of American families enjoy this stimulating life for several weeks or months each summer.

Sovereign Readi-Cut Summer Cottages are distinguished from most summer cottages by the superiority of materials and construction and, while being wonderfully low in price, give every service demanded over a long period of years. Not the least of the pleasures derived by our customers many times is that of actually erecting the cottage themselves. Their vacation is planned with the arrival of the material and the joy of creating and building *their own* cottage lends a keen appreciation to its use in future years.

The frames of all summer cottages are of good, clean No. 1 dressed lumber; of proper size and design, not greatly dissimilar to dwelling houses. The siding is practically clear Yellow Pine or Oregon Fir, tongued and grooved. The rooms are all open to the rafters, the partitions being of clear Yellow Pine or Orgeon Fir. Ceiling partition lumber finished both sides. The flooring is clear Yellow Pine or Oregon Fir.

Specifications for Sovereign Summer Cottages

The following specifications apply generally to all summer cottages, but vary slightly in some cases, according to the size of the cottage; that is, in relation to size of sills, joists, and rafters.

Foundation sills, 4 x 6 in.
Joists, 2 x 6 in.
Studding, 2 x 4 in.
Rafters, 2 x 4 in.
Siding, ⅞-in. tongued and grooved, bevel face.
Flooring, matched.
Partitions, matched ceiling.
Roof, sheathing ⅞ in.
Shingles or roofing.
Doors, windows (glazed).
Hardware, paint for two coats outside, any color, nails, locks, hinges.
No plaster or plaster board furnished.

The Asbury $144.40

Price, $152.00
Cash discount, 5%
Net price, $144.40

THE Asbury is a cosy little summer cottage of pleasing lines—built for two. The porch can be screened in to give an outdoor living room. The front door has glass in the upper portion, giving additional light to the living room. This is one of the old original summer cottages and has been erected in hundreds of towns and cities throughout the country. At price quoted you get nails, paints, glass—everything to complete the Asbury. See general summer cottage specifications above and Terms on page 2.

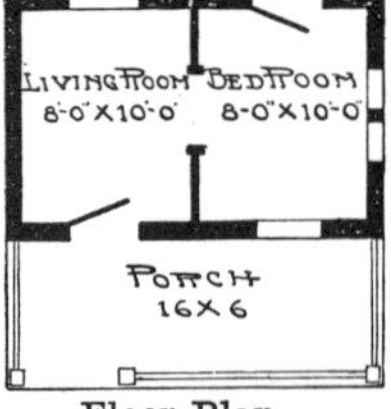

Floor Plan The Asbury

The Betcone

$297.35

Price, $313.00
Cash discount, 5%
Net price, $297.35

THE plan of The Betcone is a five-room cottage with ample porch. The three bed rooms are plenty large enough for a double bed in each. The living room is also used as a dining room. Kitchen, with rear door, is at rear. Here is one of our best sellers and always gives the greatest pleasure to owners. Easily and quickly put up. See general summer cottage specifications, page 102 and Terms on page 2.

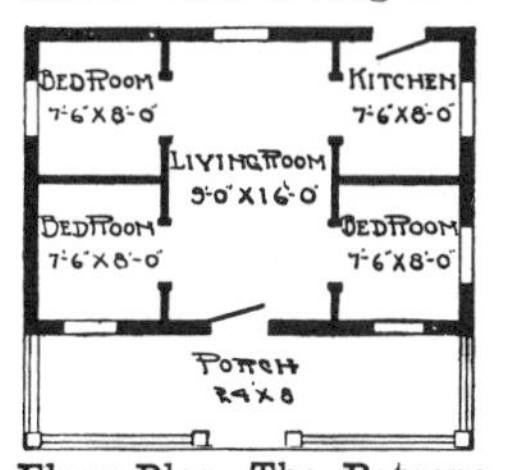

Floor Plan–The Betcone

The Genesee

$312.55

Price, $329.00
Cash discount, 5%
Net price, $312.55

WHEREVER erected this cottage has had the most favorable comment. You will save a least $150 in purchasing this cottage, and at the same time have as strongly built house as is ever erected for summer cottage purposes. Bed rooms are one side of house and dining room and kitchen on other. A splendid type of cottage. See General Specifications, page 102 and Terms on page 2.

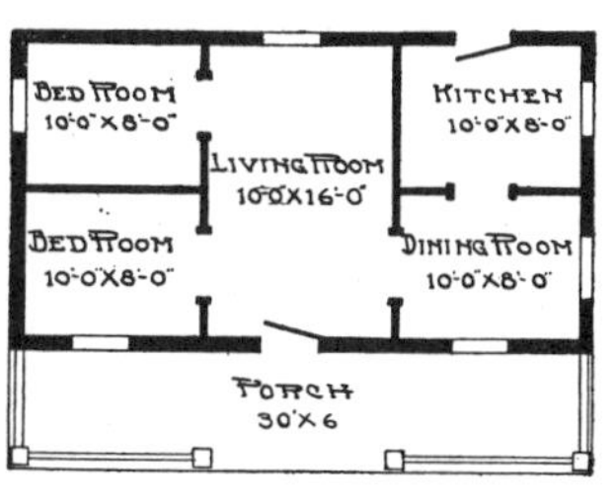

Floor Plan—The Genesee

The Statler $267.90

YOU can erect the Statler *yourself* this vacation. And you can do it in a few days' time and save the cost of carpenter work. Just the right size for the family of four or five. Plenty of ventilation throughout—bed rooms plenty large enough for double bed or two cots. The porch is large and airy, affording an opportunity for out-door sleeping. Enjoy a few days' time this vacation building *your own* summer home. See General Specifications on page 102 and Terms on page 2.

Price, $282.00
Cash discount, 5%
Net price, $267.90

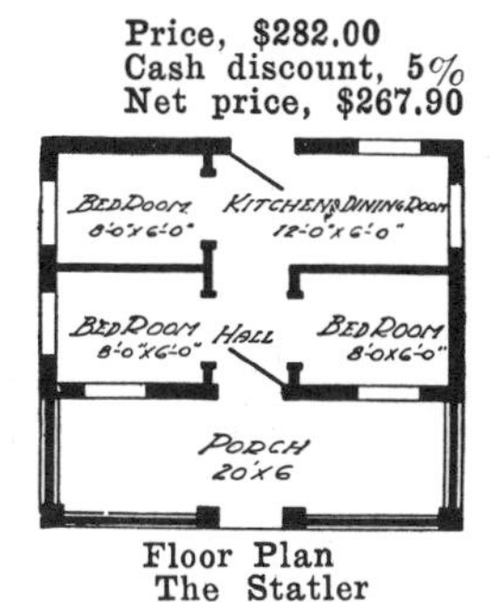

Floor Plan
The Statler

The Shoreview $294.50

Price, $310.00
Cash discount, 5%
Net price, $294.50

THE Shoreview is a comfortable summer home of five rooms. A good 10 x 16 ft. living room is located at the front. Behind the living room are two bed rooms, dining room, and kitchen, making a most complete floor plan with the porch across the front. See General Specifications on page 102 and Terms on page 2.

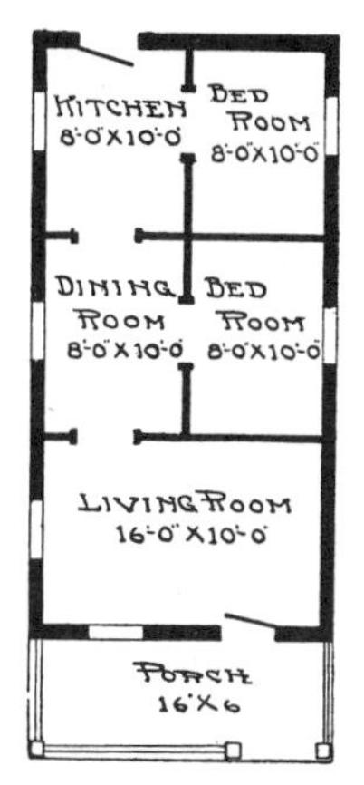

Floor Plan
The Shoreview

The Luna

$389.50

Price, $410.00
Cash discount, 5%
Net price, $389.50

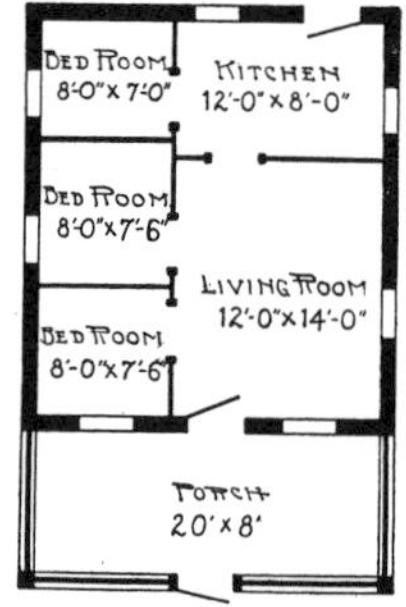

Floor Plan—The Luna

ABUNDANT space in this trim little summer cottage. Well screened porch of good size. Three sleeping rooms, living room and kitchen on inside. You will note that it can be set on a very narrow lot. Gives splendid satisfaction. See general specifications, page 102, for further information. See Terms on page 2.

The Seaford

$463.60

Price, $488.00
Cash discount, 5%
Net price, $463.60

A COSY summer home. Plenty of space on front porch—can be used for open-air dining room or sleeping room. Three bedrooms, dining room, living room and kitchen on inside. Plenty of light and air—an abundance of space. Is really one of the neatest cottages imaginable. See general summer cottage specifications, page 102 and Terms on page 2.

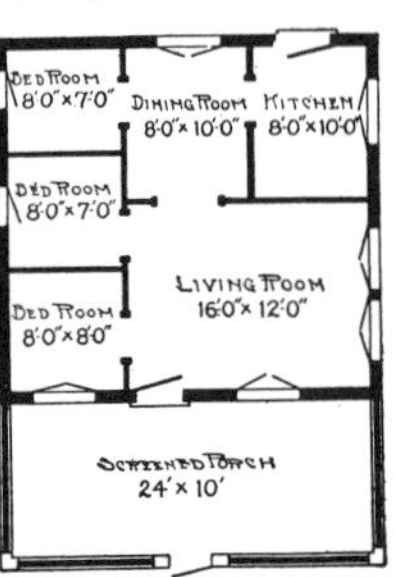

Floor Plan
The Seaford

The Drayton

$207.10

Price, $218.00
Cash discount, 5%
Net price, $207.10

THE Drayton sells for less than $210.00. When you consider that this price includes absolutely everything needed for the erection and completion of the entire building you will appreciate the surprising price. Two bed rooms can be arranged by combining living room and dining room. See General Specifications on page 102 and Terms on page 2.

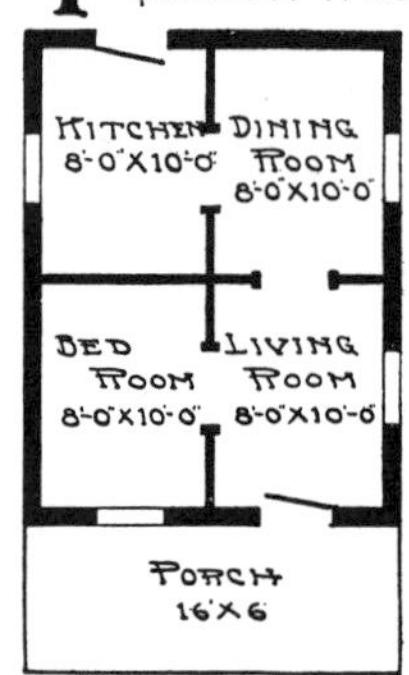

Floor Plan
The Drayton

The Shasta

$486.40

Price, $512.00
Cash discount, 5%
Net price, $486.40

A BIG summer cottage at a small price. Note the 36-ft. porch running all the way across the front of the building. Another one of our pioneer designs. Always makes a good impression and saves a good deal of money. See General Specifications, page 102 and Terms on page 2.

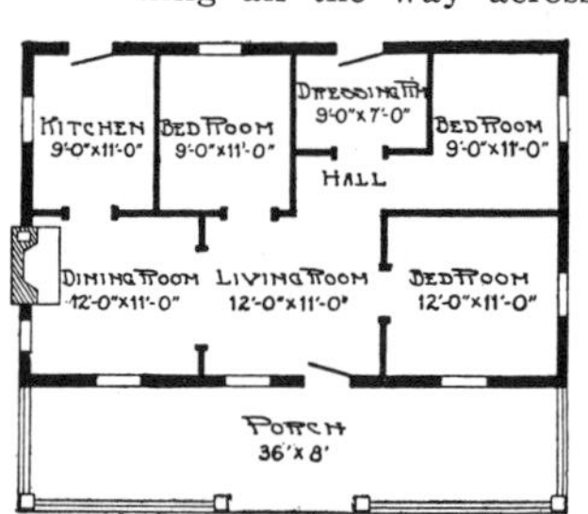

Floor Plan—The Shasta

Aladdin Hunter's Lodge

This building is designed for settler's house or hunter's lodge. It is built just like other houses, strong and substantial. One door in front and four windows, two on each side. Height of side wall, 7 ft. 6 in. No plaster board or lath and plaster are furnished with this house at the price quoted.

Size, 12 x 16 ft. Price, $133.00. Cash Discount, 5%. Net Price, $126.35. See Terms on page 2.

Popular Aladdin Garages

ALADDIN Garages are staunchly built of the same splendid grades of material entering into the construction of our dwellings. Quick shipment, simply and easily erected, paints of colors to match your house included. Walls and roof furnished in metal 25% extra. A special feature is made of quick shipment. Standard material is always carried in stock so that your garage is loaded very quickly.

The Buick $54.15

Garage Complete

ALADDIN Garages have led the market for ten years. Staunch construction, high grade material and rock bottom prices have made an irresistible appeal upon automobile owners throughout the land. The Buick, illustrated on this page, is made in two standard sizes, the 8x14 ft. size being designed for Ford cars. It is just large enough to admit a Ford touring car with the top either up or down. Any garage of smaller dimensions will not admit the Ford car. This size sells complete with all material cut to fit, paints to match the colors of your house, hardware, locks, nails and roofing at $57.00. Cash discount, 5%. Net price, $54.15.

Size 10x16 ft. is of the same construction and sells for $72.00. Cash discount, 5%. Net price, $68.40. This will admit a car of 110 inch wheel base.

All garages shown are furnished without floors, as practically all auto owners prefer to build floor of concrete.

The Winton

Size, 12x20 ft. Price, complete, $136.00. Cash Discount, 5%. Net Price, $129.20. See Terms on Page 2.

THE Winton will take the largest car on the market, with ample room at sides for working about car and for supplies. It has swinging glass doors and one window on each side. It is of a splendid type and always looks good wherever it may be erected. Painted to match your house.

The Pierce Arrow

Size, 20x18 ft. (two cars). One door. Price, $258.00. Cash Discount, 5%. Net Price, $245.10. Extra for double doors, $11. See Terms on Page 2.

THE PIERCE-ARROW is one of our most attractive garages. Will accommodate two cars without crowding. Side walls are shingled. The dormer adds much light to interior of garage. Double doors are regularly furnished. Sufficient space is available at end for work bench. Price includes paint for trim and stain for shingles.

The Maxwell

Size, 10x16 ft. Price, $117.00. Cash Discount, 5%. Net Price, $111.15. See Terms on Page 2.

A SHINGLE-COVERED Garage that nicely matches any house. Roof extends in front to afford protection during inclement weather. Eaves have exposed rafters. Good, wide double doorway. Compact, but convenient in every respect. Plenty of light.

The Peerless

Size, 20x20 ft. (two cars). One door. Price, $260.00. Cash Discount, 5%. Net Price, $247.00. Extra for double doors, $11. See Terms on Page 2.

DISTINCTIVE and attractive. The Peerless will do credit to any surroundings. It is furnished with siding half-way up and shingles on upper part of wall. Very wide eaves with supporting brackets set off building excellently. Large door with glass, together with windows on two sides, give plenty of light.

The Packard

Size, 20x20 ft. (two cars). One door. Price, $210.00. Cash Discount, 5%. Net Price, $199.50. Extra for double doors, $11. See Terms on Page 2.

Size, 30x20 ft. (three cars). Two doors. With double sliding doors. Price, $284.00. Cash Discount, 5%. Net Price, $269.80. See Terms on Page 2.

THE broken roof lines of the Packard give it an individuality immediately apparent. The building is furnished with five windows, large glass door, and small door.

Additions to Aladdin Houses

Designed for use on any House

THE additions shown on this page were designed to meet the demands which we have had in the past for additions to dwelling houses. Several different designs are shown so the purchaser may select one that will be best adapted to his requirements.

The exterior finish of these additions will be furnished to harmonize with the appearance of your house without extra cost. The prices are quoted with and without lath and plaster or plaster board, and interior finish of the enclosed part.

Addition No. 1

Addition No. 1 can be used as a kitchen with pantry, or as an extra bedroom, as desired, or will be very well adapted for an entryway, with either pantry or bath.

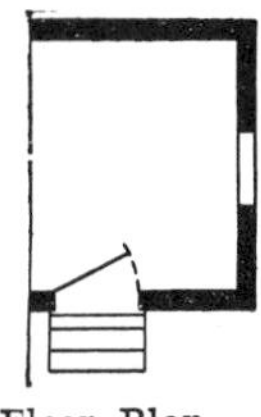

Floor Plan
Addition No. 1

Size	Net Price without Plastering	Net Price with Plastering
8 x 10	$64.00	$72.00
8 x 16	82.00	91.00
10 x 16	130.00	140.00
10 x 18	138.00	150.00
10 x 20	147.00	160.00
10 x 24	162.00	198.00

Addition No. 1

Addition No. 2

Addition No. 2 has an enclosed part, which is suitable for a pantry or bath, and has an open porch.

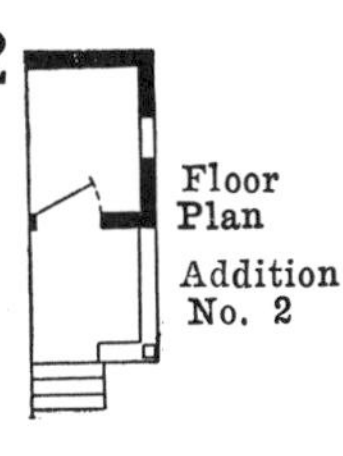

Floor Plan
Addition No. 2

Size	Net Price without Plastering	Net Price with Plastering
6x14, enclosed part, 6x 8 open part, 6x 6	$68.00	$72.00
8x16, enclosed part, 9x 8 open part, 7x 8	94.00	101.00
10x18, enclosed part, 10x10 open part, 10x 8	127.00	137.00

Addition No. 2

Addition No. 4

Addition No. 4

Addition No. 4 is a simple enclosed, rear entrance with cellar stairs. It can, of course, be attached to any house as all material necessary to complete the addition is included. Paints for two coats of any color to match balance of house as well as nails, hardware, etc., are furnished at the price quoted. See floor plan herewith. Price, net, $42.90

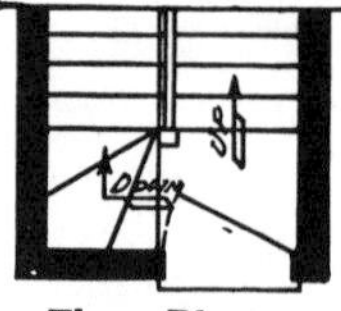

Floor Plan
Addition No. 4

Addition No. 5

Addition No. 5

To meet the popular demand for sleeping porches and sun rooms, arranged for screening in summer and sash in winter, we are offering in Additions Nos. 5 and 6 two very convenient and practical designs which have found especial favor with our customers.

The Addition No. 5 is furnished in size 10 x 6 ft., two stories high. This size is excellently adapted for average usage. The upper porch is large enough for a double bed, or two single beds, or three cots.

The popularity of the sleeping porch needs no comment here. This makes a splendid addition to any home. Screens are furnished for all openings and screen door.

The price, net, $100.00, includes paints for two coats outside, oils, stains, and varnishes for inside finish.

Any colors of paints can be furnished for outside body and trim to correspond with balance of house.

$1 A Knot Lumber

Addition No. 6

Addition No. 6

Addition No. 6 is furnished in size 14 x 7 ft. The sleeping porch will accommodate two double beds, nicely, while below you have, in addition to the open porch, an enclosed part, size 8 x 7 ft., which can be used for a pantry, bath, store, or fuel room, door to open into the enclosed part, either from porch or kitchen.

Price, net, with screens for all openings and screen door, $149.50. This price includes inside walls finished with matched material. Price also includes paints for two coats outside and oils and stains for inside finish.

Any colors of paints can be furnished to correspond with balance of house.

If enclosed part is wanted finished inside with lath and plaster, or plaster board, add $12 to above price.

Prices on glazed sash for sleeping room to be used in winter will be furnished upon application.

Aladdin Colonnades and Arches

The simplicity of the design of the Colonnade coupled with the extremely low price makes it a very popular one. Made of Yellow Pine, Oregon Fir or Red Oak, by skilled workmen. The price quoted does not include jambs or trim.

2A-60—Yellow Pine or Fir, net........**$12.85**
2A-62—Oak, net **14.50**

For Jambs and Trim add, for Yellow Pine, **$2.60**; Oak, **$3.65.**

A plain column Colonnade. For smaller homes or ones where extreme simplicity is desired. We furnish these made of Yellow Pine, Oregon Fir or Red Oak. Shipped in the white, that is, unfinished, from Bay City or Chicago.

2A-64—Yellow Pine or Fir, net...**$8.00**
2A-66—Oak, net **10.00**

For Jambs and Trim add, Yellow Pine, **$2.60**; Oak, **$3.65.**

This "Homecraft" Bookcase Arch has been used in thousands of homes and in every case has given perfect satisfaction. The cases are 2½ ft. wide, the columns 8 inches square. Made of Yellow Pine, Oregon Fir or Selected Oak, sent out unfinished, but complete with hardware and leaded glass doors, as shown.

No. 2A-1—Yellow Pine Arch......**$37.50**
No. 3A-1—Selected Oak Arch...... **40.50**

If you desire only one side of the bookcase it can be furnished at the following prices. Mention side you desire—right or left of illustrations shown here.

Yellow Pine **$20.00**
Selected Oak **21.00**

Side and head jambs and side and head casings are charged for extra as follows: Yellow Pine, **$2.60**; Selected Oak, **$3.65.**

The Colonnade illustrated to the left is very similar to our No. 2A-1, with a few details changed, principal of these being single door, plain glass and round columns in place of the square, as furnished with No. 2A-1. Furnished without jambs or trim but with hardware.

2B-70—Yellow Pine or Fir, net....**$30.50**
2B-72—Oak, net **31.50**

For Jambs and Trim add Yellow Pine, **$2.60**; Oak, **$3.65.**

Aladdin Built-in Buffets

Homecraft Built-in Buffet

A well proportioned "Homecraft" built-in side board or buffet has been very popular wherever offered. It is 4 ft. 6 in. wide and 7 ft. high, 14 in. deep. Has a bevel plate mirror back in opening over counter shelf, four drawers and one closet space in bottom section.

No. 2A-24—Yellow Pine, glazed, clear double strength glass $26.50

No. 2A-25—Yellow Pine, glazed leaded Crystal glass $28.75

No. 2A-26—Selected Oak, glazed, clear double strength glass $28.50

No. 2A-27—Selected Oak, glazed leaded Crystal glass $31.50

If side casing, base blocks and cap trim, as shown are wanted, add for Yellow Pine, 70c; Oak, $1.45.

Homecraft Built-in Buffet

A "Homecraft" Buffet which is just what the name indicates. The result of a Craftsman's labor. It stands 7 ft. high and is 5 ft. wide; depth, top section, 14 in.; bottom section, 18 in. Has four large linen drawers in center of base section and two smaller drawers on the sides, suitable for silverware, etc. One large and two small bevel plate mirrors in each buffet. Weight, 300 lbs.

No. 2A-30—Yellow Pine, glazed with clear double strength glass $37.25

No. 2A-31—Yellow Pine, glazed with leaded Crystal glass $39.00

No. 2A-32—Selected Oak, glazed with clear double strength glass $39.75

No. 2A-35—Selected Oak, glazed with leaded Crystal glass $41.75

If side casing, base blocks and cap trim, as shown, are wanted, add for Yellow Pine, 70c; Oak, $1.45.

Aladdin Homecraft Buffets

are designed with the object of giving the most convenience combined with the most artistic effects. They are made either of clear yellow pine or oak, and are sent out by us in the white, that is, unfinished. We furnish all hardware as shown. Finished glazed with leaded glass as shown or with plain double strength glass.

Size, 6 ft. 6 in. wide by 5 ft. 6 in. high; depth, 18 in. This cabinet has three large and four small drawers and two doors, three strong shelves in each side section. Best quality bevel plate glass mirror above shelf.

No. 2A-20—Yellow Pine Glazed clear double strength glass $39.75

No. 2A-21—Yellow Pine. Glazed Leaded Crystal glass $42.75

This case when finished to conform with the other woodwork in a home will harmonize with nearly any style of furniture. Price, F. O. B. shipping point; weight, 375 lbs.

No. 2A-22—Selected Oak, Glazed Double Strength glass $41.25

No. 2A-23—Selected Oak, Glazed Leaded Crystal glass $44.75

Aladdin Built-in Mantle Book Cases

The space next the fire place has long been devoted to use as a convenient nook for the book shelves. Aladdin designers have struck a happy combination in the cases illustrated here. It is planned to be adaptable to a twelve or fourteen foot room as priced by the widening or narrowing of the trim boards at sides. For anything between a fourteen foot and a sixteen foot room add $5. Note that the top of bookcase continues across the top of fireplace, incorporating the mantle shelf.

Prices of Book Cases including Mantle Shelf

No. 2A-40—As shown in photographs. Double doors, three shelves and two drawers below, one on each side, plain glass **$43.50**

No. 2A-42—Same as above, but with leaded glass **49.50**

No. 2A-44—As illustrated, but without drawers below, plain glass **34.25**

No. 2A-46—Same as No. 2A-44, but with leaded glass **40.00**

All of above prices in Yellow Pine or Fir. If desired in Oak, add **$3.00.**

Aladdin Bathroom Cabinet and Medicine Chest

A splendid combination for installation in your bathroom. Gives generous drawer space for linens, towels, bedding and the many bathroom accessories. Comes in combination with medicine chest and mirror door. The cabinet is 4 feet from floor to top, 12 inches deep and 26 inches wide. A cupboard, two narrow drawers and four wide drawers complete the cabinet, while the medicine chest at the top has strong plain mirror door and shelves inside. The whole combination is strongly built, neatly finished and easily installed.

2B-80—Price, complete with all hardware, Yellow Pine..**$21.80**

Aladdin Medicine Chest

A very convenient addition to any bathroom. Made to be placed in a recess in the wall, the face to come flush with the plaster. The complete chest includes all hardware, trim, mirror door, etc. This door has a 14x20 inch best quality French plate mirror. Size of recess required in wall is 20 inches wide, 26 inches high, 4½ inches deep. Has three adjustable wood shelves.

2B-88--Medicine Chest, each **$4.95**

$47.50 for a Complete FURNACE

$46.25 for a Complete Bathroom Outfit

Get a Copy of the ALADDIN Book of Merchandise

A complete heating plant for any ordinary home for only $47.50. Guaranteed to heat any home containing 15,000 cu. ft. of air space, or less. This is not an experiment but a demonstrated success. Many thousands of them in operation all over the country—no doubt in your city. If you need a furnace let us tell you about this one or any other kind of a heating plant that you prefer.

Above we show one of our popular electric fixture combinations which contains complete fixtures for a seven-room home, (nine fixtures in all), the price for this combination finished in any of the standard finishes is $22.00. We show many other combinations in our catalog, some less and some more expensive than this. Priced complete in sets or singly for those who do not wish a complete set.

Only one of our modern bathroom combinations. The price for this is $46.25. We show a most complete line of bathroom fixtures and modern plumbing appliances of all kinds. If you are building you cannct afford to be without our Merchandise Catalog.

Send for Your Copy Today

ORDER TO

THE ALADDIN COMPANY

BAY CITY, MICHIGAN

Your money will be instantly returned if what you purchase from us is not found to be entirely satisfactory in every particular and exactly as represented. Safe arrival of all material is guaranteed.

W. J. Sovereign President

THE ALADDIN CO.

The following order is placed under the absolute guarantee of complete satisfaction to purchaser, which is printed above.

INSTRUCTIONS FOR SHIPPING MY HOUSE

Date ______________________

Ship to ______________________

Street ______________________ Town ______________________

County ______________________ State ______________________

Via ______________________ R. R. Is there a Freight Agent there? ______________________

ORDERED BY ______________________

Street ______________________ Town ______________________

County ______________________ State ______________________

Enclosed please find $ ______________________ for which ship me at once

TEAR HERE

Style of House ______________________ Shown on Catalog Page ______________________

SIDING OR SHINGLES For Outside Walls ______________________

LATH AND PLASTER OR PLASTER BOARD For Inside Walls ______________________

SHINGLES OR ROOFING For Roof ______________________

What Kind of a Foundation will you Use? ______________________

Color Paint or Stain for Side Walls ______________________ Trim ______________________

Color Porch Floor ______________________

Inside Finish ______________________

EXACT WORDS OF OWNERS

New York.

Would say I am more than pleased with my Kentucky bungalow which is built on Laurel Ave. It comes up to all the requirements of my needs. A number of my friends wonder how a bungalow like it can be cut at the factory and then constructed; or as you say, Readi-cut. But I can understand it as I am a carpenter. Am enclosing two views of my bungalow.

EDWARD C. SAYRE.

Ohio.

I am very thankful to say I am well pleased with my house in every respect. We are now comfortably fixed up with all modern conveniences and you can think of us as a happy little family in a beautiful, little Aladdin bungalow. So many others could be proud owners of Aladdin homes if they only knew what a good, honest firm you are to deal with. You surely have been loyal to me in every respect and if I ever build again I will prove to you I appreciate your interest and kindness.

J. L. SANDERS.

Ohio.

I am sending you a small picture of the 2 "Denver" bungalows we got from you over a year ago. We had some very cold weather last winter but were kept very comfortable in our new homes. They were very easy to keep warm. We are still improving our homes and when we get them up to our ideas we will send you good pictures of them.

Yours truly,
J. L. and H. W. SANDERS.

Indiana.

We are glad to recommend you to others, as we are so well satisfied with our house and all our dealings with you. We have had so many to admire our little cottage the "Chester" and are very proud of it. All the material was "No. 1," every piece fitted well and saved carpenters bills. ORUS J. WHITE.

Pennsylvania.

I think the Aladdin Readi-cut system is the only way to build a house, because you save a lot on both labor and lumber. I saved at least $500.00 on my house. People came to see it from a distance of 60 miles and all liked it very much. I am always glad to show it to anyone as I am proud of it. Ours is the Oakland bungalow. Yours very truly,

CLAYTON W. FARBER.

Ohio.

We surely are pleased with our Maples bungalow and cannot say enough to praise it. Everything fit fine and am pleased to say I saved between $600.00 and $700.00 in building by the readi-cut method. Yours respectfully,

FRED WENT.

Ohio.

The material in my Winthrop was just as represented and I am well pleased with it in every way. I have considered neither time nor workmanship on it and it has gone together perfectly. The painter told me that he found the joints more perfect in this house than any he has ever worked on and he has painted some of the highest priced ones in this city. I assure you that anyone who wishes to see it will be allowed that privilege. I estimate that I saved more than $300.00 on my home. Yours truly, H. W. SIEFER.

Oklahoma.

I am more than pleased with my "Forsyth" bungalow. The carpenters didn't use a saw in putting up the frame and everything went together perfectly. It is an ideal little home—not only a house. Everyone who has seen it praises the beautiful finishing lumber.

We only had the pleasure of living in our Aladdin three months when I was called to this city where I am teaching. I hope in the next few years I can build another Aladdin. There's a pleasure or pride which accompanies the Aladdin home that we cannot get away from. I figure I saved $600.00 by building by this method. THOS. R. STEMEN.

Massachusetts.

I have found everything in all my dealings with you just as represented and I also know for a fact that on the lumber bill alone I saved easily $500.00. All the lumber was there and had plenty of everything. I shall take great pleasure in showing my bungalow, the "Burbank" to others and feel ready to recommend you to all.

Yours truly,
GEO. S. HARDY.

Maryland.

My Denver is completed and to say that I am pleased is putting it very mild indeed. My house is built upon a knoll and raised three feet above ground. The picture in the catalog entirely fails to do it justice. During its construction it was visited and watched by scores of people and was fairly commented upon by our local newspaper on two occasions as to its appearance and the material entering into its construction. "Denver" is the password and all is well.

PATRICK REEDY.

Pennsylvania.

We believe our "Marsden" is second to none; are more than satisfied both with the house and your Golden Rule business methods. We wish you increasing prosperity. If we were to build again, we would surely have another Aladdin. J. A. McHUGH.

Pennsylvania.

My experience in building my Rochester has been very beneficial to me, not only from a financial viewpoint, but from a practical side, as I have followed the mode of construction from foundation up, and tried to find the weak points with the result that I can truly say that neither my carpenters or myself can say today that there are any. The entire transaction was completed in a pleasant businesslike way and I feel assured we are mutually benefited by same. Your method of dealing with a customer makes it impossible to be anything else than genuine boosters for Aladdin. T. J. McDERMOTT.

Indiana.

I have just finished building one of your Readi-cut houses, the Stanhope, and want to express my gratitude to you for making it possible for a poor man to have a home. Having made a personal investigation and inspection of the Ready-cut houses of the largest mail orders in the world, I am satisfied that the Aladdin Readi-cut material is far superior to theirs and the prices the most reasonable.

Rev. C. C. CRIPE.

ALADDIN Built-In Fixtures

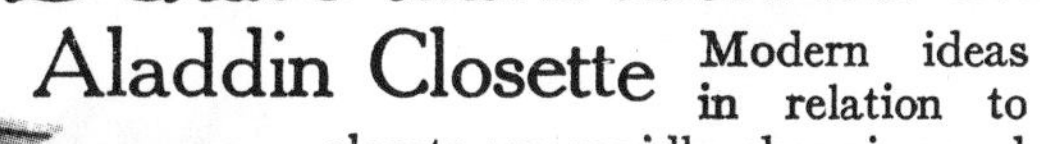

Modern ideas in relation to closets are rapidly changing and while the housewife has always spoken of the need of good closet room, a little reflection will disclose the surprising fact that most closets devote nearly three-quarters of the space to doors, elbow room and ability to walk into them, and one-quarter of the space to actual storage and hanging space.

Isn't that exactly true?

Aladdin discovered this fact in his continuous hunt for economy and waste-saving. Now then, here is a practical plan that utilizes just 4½ square feet of floor space and yet gives more hanging space and storage space than the usual four by six foot closet that occupies 24 square feet of floor space! Think of it!

And how much more convenient it is than entering a dark closet and rummaging around among hooks and shelves!

By the use of coat hooks, costing about 5 cents a dozen at notion stores, it is easily possible to hang twelve suits or robes in this space, each one being easily found and removed. Can greater capacity be gained in the average good sized closet? Above the large compartment is space for hats, bedding or other things of like character, and below a wide, deep space for shoes and the many other articles that may require a place out of the way.

The cabinet is six feet high and as in many instances, it can be inset into the bedroom wall, so that it utilizes the six inches of wall thickness and really takes up but *one foot of bedroom floor space!*

Counting the combined shelf space, it gains 13½ square feet while actually using but the aforementioned six square feet of floor space.

The photograph on this page shows the Aladdin craftsman buffet, with the white enamel finish conforming to the white woodwork of this particular room. This buffet is very roomy, having four sets of shelves with divided light glass door for each section and five drawers for linen and silver. The two drawers at the bottom are especially large for use as table-cloth receptacles.

Aladdin Buffet, size 4 ft. 6 in. by 7 ft. high by 1 ft. 6 in. deep, net................................ **$33.00**

Bay City, Michigan
ALADDIN Town
Every house shown in the Aladdin catalog is erected in Bay City with two or three exceptions. This includes all of the largest, The Villa, The Brentwood, The Colonial and The Lamberton.
You will find whole streets of Aladdin Houses, whole subdivisions on which only Aladdin Houses are erected.
Bay City is truly called Aladdin Town, and Bay City people seem very proud of it.
A most interesting trip could be arranged visiting the Aladdin Mills and inspecting the Aladdin Homes in Bay City.
Anyone planning on coming to Bay City or vicinity is earnestly invited to call on us while here.
THE ALADDIN COMPANY

WM. L. CLEMENTS, PRESIDENT
A. E. BOUSFIELD, VICE PRESIDENT
N. A. EDDY VICE PRESIDENT
F. P. BROWNE, VICE PRESIDENT
IRVING H. BAKER CASHIER
PIERCE A. McCOMBS, ASST. CASHIER

ORGANIZED 1864

2853

THE FIRST NATIONAL BANK

CAPITAL $200 000.00
SURPLUS $200 000.00

BAY CITY, MICH.

Dec. 1, 1916.

To Aladdin Customers:

We are pleased to testify to our confidence in the Aladdin Company, and to assure you that any confidence you extend them will be honorably treated.

The men behind this organization, who are perfectly responsible financially and otherwise, are all personally known to us, as is their integrity and upright business policy.

This company originated, perfected and established the Readi-Cut system of Construction, and is the pioneer as well as the largest manufacturer of houses that we know of.

You may have full confidence that the representations of this company will be fully lived up to.

Very truly yours,

Irving H. Baker

Cashier.

INDEX